Understanding Your Students' Religions

This concise guide helps educators understand the diverse religious practices that shape students' school and home lives. Using an encyclopedia-like structure, the authors provide short histories and other essential information on a wide variety of religions as well as atheist practices.

Each chapter covers origins, beliefs, practices, and common misunderstandings and stereotypes, as well as key holidays, religious dress, and dietary restrictions that can be accommodated in school. This book will help educators avoid stumbling over stereotypes so they can better engage students and their families and foster culturally responsive classrooms. Teachers of all grade levels will come away feeling more confident about identifying areas of cultural and religious practice where support for your students may be needed.

You will also have the tools to recognize the diversity of religious and cultural practices that students bring to the classroom, and to see that unfamiliar religious and cultural practices are assets to be cultivated and not signs of deficiency.

Liz Wilson has published on South Asian forms of sexual regulation, especially celibacy, South Asian modes of death and dying, and how Asian foodways and modes of religious dress have been adopted and altered in Western contexts. She has published a monograph on how gender figures in Buddhist literature about meditation, two edited volumes on Asian religious practices, and a coauthored textbook on religion, gender, and the body. Wilson teaches a course on religion and law that deals with case law on non-Christian religious expression in U.S. schools.

Michael Nichols specializes in Asian religions and religion in popular culture. He has published a monograph on Buddhist mythology and another monograph on the Marvel comic cinematic universe as seen through the lens of religious studies.

Peter W. Williams is an expert on American religions, with a particular focus on material culture and religious architecture. He has published a monograph on popular religion in America, another book on religion and architecture in America, and a reference work on America's religions that has been a perennial source of information for many different audiences.

Also Available from Routledge Eye on Education

www.routledge.com/k-12

Identity Affirming Classrooms: Spaces that Center Humanity
Erica Buchanan-Rivera

Culturally Responsive Education in the Classroom: An Equity Framework for Pedagogy
Adeyemi Stembridge

Culturally Responsive Teaching in Gifted Education: Building Cultural Competence and Serving Diverse Student Populations
Edited By C. Matthew Fugate, Wendy A. Behrens, Cecelia Boswell, and Joy Lawson Davis

Is Your Lesson for You or Your Students? A Framework for Student-Centered, Culturally Responsive, and Aligned Instruction
Jahkari H. Taylor

Let's Get Real, Second Edition: Exploring Race, Class, and Gender Identities in the Classroom
Martha Caldwell and Oman Frame

Understanding Your Students' Religions
A Guide to Culturally Responsive Practices

Liz Wilson, Michael Nichols,
and Peter W. Williams

Routledge
Taylor & Francis Group

NEW YORK AND LONDON

Designed cover image: Getty Images

First published 2025
by Routledge
605 Third Avenue, New York, NY 10158

and by Routledge
4 Park Square, Milton Park, Abingdon, Oxon, OX14 4RN

Routledge is an imprint of the Taylor & Francis Group, an informa business

© 2025 Liz Wilson, Michael Nichols, and Peter W. Williams

The right of Liz Wilson, Michael Nichols, and Peter W. Williams, and to be identified as authors of this work has been asserted in accordance with sections 77 and 78 of the Copyright, Designs and Patents Act 1988.

All rights reserved. No part of this book may be reprinted or reproduced or utilised in any form or by any electronic, mechanical, or other means, now known or hereafter invented, including photocopying and recording, or in any information storage or retrieval system, without permission in writing from the publishers.

Trademark notice: Product or corporate names may be trademarks or registered trademarks, and are used only for identification and explanation without intent to infringe.

ISBN: 978-1-032-52278-4 (hbk)
ISBN: 978-1-032-51564-9 (pbk)
ISBN: 978-1-003-40589-4 (ebk)

DOI: 10.4324/9781003405894

Typeset in Palatino
by codeMantra

Contents

Acknowledgments x
Meet the Authors xi

1 Why Care About Religion? Principles of Religious Literacy 1

2 African Diaspora Religions 6

3 Atheist, Agnostic, Humanist, and Anti-Religious Groups 16

4 Baha'i 30

5 Buddhism 34

6 Chinese Religions: Falun Gong 45

7 Chinese Religions: Traditional Chinese Religions 51

8 Christianity: Overview 62

9 Christianity: Amish, Mennonite, and Other Anabaptist-Descended Churches 69

10 Christianity: Anglican and Episcopal 74

11 Christianity: Baptist 79

12 Christianity: Black Churches 87

13 Christianity: Christian Science 92

14 Christianity: Jehovah's Witnesses 95

15 Christianity: Latter-Day Saints 97

16 Christianity: Lutherans 101

17 Christianity: Methodist, Moravian, Wesleyan, and
    Holiness Churches 106

18 Christianity: Orthodox 111

19 Christianity: Pentecostal and Holiness 116

20 Christianity: Presbyterian and Other Reformed
    Churches. 120

21 Christianity: Quakers (Friends) 125

22 Christianity: Restorationist (Churches of Christ,
    Disciples of Christ) 128

23 Christianity: Roman and Eastern Catholic 131

24 Christianity: Seventh-day Adventists 140

25 Christianity: Unitarian Universalist. 143

26 Hinduism: Overview 146

27 Hinduism: Shaiva. 160

28 Hinduism: Shakta. 162

29 Hinduism: Vaishnava 164

30 Islam: Overview 166

31 Islam: The Nation of Islam. 175

32 Islam: Shia 178

33 Islam: Sunni. 180

34 Jainism 183

35 Judaism: Overview 186

36 Judaism: Conservative 192

37 Judaism: Orthodox 195

38 Judaism: Reform 199

39 Neo-Paganism 203

40 North American Indigenous Religions 209

41 Scientology 217

42 Sikhism. 220

43 Zoroastrianism 231

Acknowledgments

Liz Wilson appreciates John Charles Duffy for his help in thinking through the shape of this book and in reading draft chapters. She thanks Allan Smith for reading draft chapters and offering useful comments.

Michael Nichols would like to thank his coauthors, Liz Wilson and Peter Williams, as well as Melinda Zook and Stephanie Ayala-Chittick at Purdue for their support, and the Humanities, Social Sciences, and Education (HSSE) Library at Purdue for providing necessary background sources for his chapters.

Peter Williams gratefully acknowledges the assistance of:

Curtis Ellison
John Erickson
Hillel Gray
Nancy Jo Kemper
Scott Kenworthy
Charles Lippy
Lisa Poirier
Daniel Sack
Grant Wacker
Charles Wallace

Meet the Authors

Liz Wilson is Professor at Miami University. She is the coauthor (with M. Wilcox and N. Hoel) of *Religion, The Body, and Sexuality* (2019) and author of *Charming Cadavers: Horrific Figurations of the Feminine in Indian Buddhist Hagiographic Literature* (1996), in addition to other scholarly publications.

Michael Nichols is Assistant Teaching Professor at Purdue University. He is the author of two books: *Religion and Myth in the Marvel Cinematic Universe* (2021) and *Malleable Mara: Transformations of a Buddhist Symbol of Evil* (2019). He is the recipient of teaching excellence awards from Saint Joseph's College and Purdue University.

Peter W. Williams is University Distinguished Professor of Comparative Religion and American Studies Emeritus at Miami University. He is the author of, among other books, *Religion, Art, and Money: Episcopalians and American Culture from the Civil War to the Great Depression* (2015) and coeditor of the *Encyclopedia of Religion in America* (2010).

1

Why Care About Religion? Principles of Religious Literacy

Why Care about Religion?

Religion is an anxiety-ridden topic for many in American public schools. Legislation limiting religious activities in schools and court rulings that circumscribe how religion is taught in public schools naturally cause anxiety among teachers and administrators. School textbooks often avoid the subject of religion altogether. Some teachers and administrators might be inclined to take the path of avoidance, leaving religion out of the curriculum altogether. Others recognize that students need to learn about the religious landscape of the United States, but lack the resources to develop lessons. This book is designed to offer resources on that landscape for teachers, administrators, and others inside and outside schools who seek information about the way that religion is practiced by various people in the United States. It's designed to be a resource that can be quickly consulted to answer a question about a student's religious practices. Has a Seventh-day Adventist student enrolled in your school? This book will let you know about the vegetarian diet that is common among this group of Christians so that cafeteria staff can address the student's needs promptly. There are others outside schools for whom this book could be useful. Healthcare workers, journalists, social workers, and many others who encounter unfamiliar religious affiliations among the people they encounter in their work can use this resource to become more knowledgeable about the practices and beliefs of their clients.

Religious Literacy

The diversity of religion in America is astounding. While America has always been a land of immigrants, our demographic profile changed radically in the twentieth century. In the 1960s, the U.S. policy that barred immigration to certain groups (such as Asians) was scrapped and new legislation opened up channels of immigration to people from Asia, Africa, and the Middle East. Communities of Hindus, Muslims, and practitioners of Afro-Caribbean religions have become established in towns and cities all over the country. But unfortunately knowledge of the religious dimensions of non-Christian communities lags far behind the reality of twenty-first-century American life. And even when it comes to Christianity, it is often surprising how little Americans actually know, beyond a thin tissue of stereotypes. Religions are deeply embedded in many spheres of life – personal, social, political, and cultural. Imagine studying art history without knowing anything about religion. The very idea is absurd. Religion has functioned throughout human history as something that inspires humans to act in various ways. For example, it often motivates people at the ballot box, as they elect leaders, and inspires them to fight for certain causes and align themselves with certain groups. Given how religion shapes the way we view the world and how it has inspired many powerful social movements and lasting institutions, everyone should be literate in the religious dimensions of human experience. Religious literacy is not just knowledge for the sake of knowledge, but has many practical applications. If more workplaces were run by religiously literate employers, worker satisfaction could be improved. But of all the groups that can benefit from religious literacy, educators stand out.

Culturally Responsive Pedagogy

Educators should appreciate that religion is a key factor that shapes the lives of students. Religion doesn't just shape the lives of students outside of school. A student's religious life can be a learning resource inside the school. Since religions are different, religions equip students to learn in different ways. Culturally responsive pedagogy suggests that students' religious and ethnic identities yield different ways of approaching the task of learning. Some religions, for example, center textual learning and value memorization. Students who practice these religions are likely to thrive when assignments require memorizing vast amounts of material. Other religions stress the importance of storytelling and imagination, giving students who practice these religions an advantage when assignments ask for creativity and narrative expansiveness. Instead of being something to be feared as divisive, religion should be seen as a potential asset in the classroom, if educators take the time to unlock the resources that religion offers to student learning.

Is It Legally Permissible to Teach about Religion in Public Institutions?

While the sectarian practice of religion is not appropriate, the U.S. Supreme Court has judged the academic study of religion to be constitutionally sound. Our book is *not* meant to be a primer on how religious studies should be taught in primary and secondary school settings. This book is intended to offer a quick guide that can help educators understand the practices that shape the home lives of students as well as the ways that religious dress, dietary practices, and other behaviors can shape how students operate in U.S. school settings. It is intended as a diversity training primer on religious and cultural pluralism in U.S. elementary and secondary schools. But part of what it means to be a culturally responsive educator is to allow discussion of religion into the classroom. It is our belief that in order to enrich classroom experiences for all students and especially for students who practice non-dominant religions, educators need to bring religion into their classrooms in a culturally responsive way.

What's Included Here

In a slim volume like this one, we obviously could not cover all aspects of the religious landscape in America today. To select the religions chosen, we asked questions like these: Is the religion currently practiced in the United States? Does it have national adherence or merely local? Will it figure significantly among students in the public school system in the United States? Is it likely to shape the lives of students in significant ways during the school day?

Once we established the list of religions we wished to include, other questions had to be tackled. What aspects of a religion are most important for the readers of this book to know about? Do readers need to understand the historical pathways that led to the development of the religions showcased here? How much attention should be given to the differences of belief and practice with any given religion – the complexities of sect and subsect that characterize some of the religions covered here? Our guiding principle has been to ask whether this information affects the day-to-day practice of the religion and to include it only where it seems likely to impinge on the practice of the religion in school settings. When possible, we have condensed the histories and origin stories of the religions covered in this book in favor of information that will shed light on what a teacher or administrator might encounter in a classroom setting. The accent here is on what would be useful in classroom settings. We know that fear of making a mistake can be quite inhibiting for school personnel who wish to understand how religion figures in the lives of their students. Thus we address common misunderstandings and stereotypes so that educators can be confident of the assumptions they make about religion. It's disappointing that so many educators avoid the question of religion. It's not only one of the things that shapes the lives of students, but it's a learning asset that can be tapped. Culturally responsive pedagogy suggests that students' religious and ethnic identities constitute important learning resources. This book details specific skills and propensities that different religions give students. It shows how such skills can be cultivated, giving examples of exercises that educators might assign to take advantage of these religion-based potentialities.

Chapter Format

Each chapter is subdivided into sections that are consistent across all entries: Opening Vignette, Introduction, Historical Overview, Main Subgroups, Scriptures, Festivals, Common Misunderstandings, Stereotypes, and Classroom Concerns, Further Reading and Resources. (Some entries required fewer sections, so there is some variation across entries.) In this way, the reader will be able to use this book as a resource for getting information efficiently. Common subdivisions will allow the reader to compare facts about different religions.

Terminology

We have avoided the diacritics used to transcribe in English the ways that foreign terms are pronounced. Those marks would be an unhelpful distraction in a book that is designed for non-specialists. In some cases, there are a number of different ways that a foreign term we used was rendered into English. Where decisions need to be made, we chose the most common renderings. As needed, we have provided information on pronunciation in parentheses.

2

African Diaspora Religions

> In New York City, a young woman who wants to start her own business consults a diviner, who does a divination for her with cowrie shells (delicate oval seashells). The young woman is asked questions about her situation. The diviner casts the shells onto a table and interprets how they fall, doing several throws. In the end, the young woman is told which sacred being can best assist her in establishing her business and what sacrifices would be appropriate to offer to this deity.

Introduction

It's estimated that there are over 100 million people in the world who practice religions associated with the African diaspora. These are religions that originated in Africa but were transplanted and transmuted by voluntary immigration and the movement of enslaved peoples out of Africa into areas like the Caribbean and other parts of North America, Europe, and other parts of the world. Taken together, these religious traditions make up one of the world's largest ten religions.

Historical Overview

In all the places where enslaved people were brought from Africa, they brought religious practices such as divination, initiation, healing techniques, and ceremonial worship through dancing, chanting, and music (especially music that features stylized drumming). In these ceremonies, sacred beings often make themselves present to people in the form of spirit possession. While the sacred beings worshipped in such ceremonies bear many characteristics of African deities, deified ancestors, and spirits, it was not always possible to worship African sacred beings openly, especially for enslaved people. In many parts of the New World, enslaved people were encouraged to practice Christianity. Slave owners reasoned that an enslaved person would be more loyal to owners if they shared a common religion. And the Christian religion was thought to offer moral guidance that would be conducive to docility in enslaved peoples. In those places where enslaved people practiced Roman Catholicism, the pantheon of Catholic saints proved to be a useful addition to African diaspora religious practices. Sacred beings of African origin were identified with specific Catholic saints. Altars of worship might contain objects associated with African-derived sacred beings and pictures of Catholic saints. In areas where it was not safe to practice African diaspora religions, the images of saints served to make African diaspora religion possible. But the conflation of African sacred beings and Roman Catholic saints was not just a device to enable African diaspora religion to be done in inhospitable environments. As beings with similar powers and spheres of influence, Catholic saints and African sacred beings inspire similar forms of reverence.

African diaspora religions do not rely on sacred texts but rather are passed down by word of mouth. Initiation is an important feature of these religions. It is through initiation that people learn about the ways to best serve sacred beings and to maintain the links between humans and the realm of the sacred. Initiated people are the bedrock of African diaspora religions. Initiation brings obligations to the sacred beings and to other initiated practitioners. These connections to other initiated practitioners are conceived as familial ties of godparent and godchild. Hence religious family forms the core of African diaspora religions. This kinship model operates differently than the organizational forms associated with many Christian churches. There is no centralized authority in African diaspora religions as there is in many forms of Christianity. Religious authority is more diffuse. For example, non-initiated people might visit a variety of diviners and healers but feel themselves bound to none in particular. Likewise, an initiated person might feel a strong sense of loyalty to his or her spiritual godparents but have relatively loose ties to religious leaders outside his or her immediate spiritual family. In recent years, however, some African diaspora religious congregations have begun to model themselves on the organizational style of Christian churches. This is especially the case for those groups who are applying to the U.S. government for the status of a religion.

Major Groups

Candomblé. This religion is centered around African deities and deified ancestors known in Brazil as Orixas (Orishas, in other Afro-Caribbean religions). Brazil received more enslaved people than any other region in the world during the era of the Atlantic slave trade. Enslaved people came from various parts of Africa. The deities that they brought with them were mingled and consolidated, based on ongoing relevance, into the pantheon of Brazilian Orixas. Candomblé practitioners honor a supreme creator; the Orixas serve as intermediaries between humans and the creator. Each individual is assigned an Orixa who is associated with a certain disposition, a specific color, a particular type of food, and certain elements of nature. People serve the Orixas through ceremonial dancing, singing, and chanting. Orixas make themselves available to people at such gatherings by spirit possession. The Orixas only appear through the medium of initiated people. Possessed persons put on clothing and carry objects representing the Orixa in question. They offer predictions and communicate with the congregation through stylized dancing and verbal exchanges.

Initiation is a gateway to the highest levels of service to the Orixas. Initiation is more common for women than men, especially in Brazil. Initiations can be expensive. They involve seclusion, austere living, the removal of everyday clothing, the shaving of head hair and/or body hair, and the learning of rituals that are required to serve the Orixas.

Candomblé gives pride of place to healing ceremonies. Illness, believed to result from disequilibrium with the world of the Orixas, requires divination to reveal the underlying cause of the malady. Once the causes are known, spiritual cleansing is required. This can entail bathing in water infused with healing vegetation or rubbing plants on the skin. Spiritual cleaning often requires sacrifices to specific Orixas. Patients drink teas made from healing herbs and apply powders. In some cases, it's deemed that healing cannot occur unless the sufferer undergoes initiation.

Holidays

- ♦ The annual festival days of the Orixas are held on the feast days of the saints corresponding to the Orixas.
- ♦ Yemanjá's day (February 2) is one of the most popular of the Orixas' birthdays. Devotees load boats with offerings to her and then cast the offerings out into the water.

Santeria. This is a Spanish word (translating as "the way of the saints") that refers to a group of traditions that developed in the nineteenth-century Cuba before making a home in the United States in the twentieth and twenty-first centuries. This tradition is also called Lukumi (or Lucumi) and Regle de Ocho.

Practitioners can be found especially in metropolitan centers like Miami and New York City. Among immigrants from Cuba, there are many who didn't practice Afro-Caribbean religions while living in Cuba but have adopted this way of practice in the United States. Santeria offers immigrants living in novel and challenging environments ways to cope, to heal, and to restore justice when the legal system cannot deliver. Although some scholars characterize African diaspora religions as religions of the poor, fieldwork done in New York City in the 1980s showed practitioners of Santeria to be predominantly middle-class people, including teachers, social workers, and other professionals.

The Santeria religion has its roots in the religious practices of the Yoruba people living in what is now Nigeria. The worship of Orishas, or holy beings, can be traced back to Yoruba practices brought to Cuba and hybridized with Catholic saints and sacred beings indigenous to Cuba. Through drumming and dancing, practitioners communicate with the Orishas. Orishas make themselves present to their worshippers through spirit possession. In worship ceremonies, initiated members of the congregation enter into altered states with the assistance of ceremonial drumming and engage in dialogue with the congregation, answering questions and giving solace.

Animal blood is offered to Orisha icons in some rituals, a practice that has led to conflict with local authorities and animal rights groups. The practice has been reviewed and ratified as constitutionally protected. In a case that went to the Supreme Court in the early 1900s, a city in the suburbs of Miami, Florida, passed a number of ordinances that struck members of a local Santeria congregation as amounting to suppression of their religion. They fought their way through various legal channels, finally to have the justices of the Supreme Court support their first amendment rights.

When people practicing Santeria are in poor health (mental or physical) or suffering difficult circumstances, they use divination to determine what is obstructing balance. They reach out ceremonially to incite the Orishas, thereby hoping to re-balance their lives and restore order. Santeria congregations contain members with different levels of access to the Orisha based on different levels of initiation. Initiation endows people with a more potent spiritual condition and gives them the capacity to act as priests and priestesses. Extended spiritual families are created as priests initiate people and take on the role of godparents for those people. Those people can initiate others, who treat as family both their initiating godparents and the godparents of their godparents.

Holidays

- Feast of **Obatala**, the creator. September 24.
- Feast of **Babalu Aye**, god of healing. December 17.

Vodou (Voodoo) is a Haitian religion that blends African and European influences. Women leaders play key roles in this variety of Afro-Caribbean religious practices. They preside over spiritual families, conduct ceremonies, manufacture charms, and attend to powerful ancestors. Devotees serve African-born spirits who join congregants at ritual dances. Vodou practitioners recognize a supreme being who is served by a pantheon of spirits known as **lwa** or *loa*. The lwa pantheon includes key African deities, deified ancestors, and embodiments of Catholic saints. The pantheon includes helpful, kind spirits and tempestuous, ambivalent ones. Together, the lwa offer protection, healing, and guidance. Grateful devotees serve the lwa in individual and collective rituals. A person will wear clothing associated with certain lwa, feed the lwa, and arrange for sacrifices as needed. Group ceremonies involve singing, drumming, dancing, prayer, special foods, animal sacrifices, altars, and candles. The lwa make themselves available to their devotees through spirit possession. When this occurs, the devotee possessed by the lwa is treated as vehicle for the spirit and referred to as a horse that is mounted by the lwa. They wear special clothing and carry items associated with the spirit in question. The possessed individual communicates messages from the lwa through stylized dances and evocative phrases.

Initiation ceremonies are common, often involving dancing, head and foot washing, and clothing changes.

Holidays

- Saint John's Eve. Very popular in New Orleans, ceremony of feasting.
- Day of the Dead, All Saints Day, All Souls Day. Important days for the worship of spirits associated with the dead, especially the raucous, fun-loving spirits who typically arrive late in the course of all-night ceremonies, rousing devotees from lethargy.

Rastafari (Rastafarianism). Rastafari is a religious and political movement of Afro-Jamaican origin. It was established in 1932, with the crowning of Ras (King) Tafari Makonnen as the emperor of the Ethiopian Kingdom. This event was a boon to the pan-Africanist movement, since the Ethiopian Kingdom was one of only two sovereign nations in Africa at the time. Jamaica native Marcus Mosiah Garvey was a leading figure in this movement. Teaching his followers to cultivate racial pride through identification with African civilization, the followers of Garvey initiated a movement that was fed by pan-African politics, folk Christianity, and Afrocentric interpretations of Judaism. The emperor of the Ethiopian Kingdom, who changed his name to Haile Selassie, plays a central role as a divine figure and source of the divinity of all Black people.

Achieving a balance with nature is one of the central tenets of the religion. Rastas decry the use of synthetic materials and generally avoid cigarettes, alcohol, and hard drugs. Rastas avoid pork and shellfish, in keeping with the Biblical book of Leviticus, and many Rastas follow a vegetarian lifestyle. Holy herbs such as ganja (marijuana) are said to be given by God for healing and used ceremonially. Many Rastas prefer African-style clothing. Dreadlocks are common in Rasta communities as marks of connection with God and a commitment to a natural lifestyle. Collective worship involves drumming, dancing, and chanting, but individual worship is also common.

The migration of Jamaicans to the United States brought Rastafari practices to North America in the 1960s and 1970s. Rastas have established schools, community centers, tabernacles, urban farms for producing their own food, and stores that feature natural lifestyle products. Reggae musicians such as Bob Marley have amplified Rasta themes on an international scale. Many Americans have learned about Rastafari themes through listening to the songs of Marley and other highly successful Reggae musicians.

Holidays

- Haile Selassie's birthday, July 23.
- Crowning of Emperor Haile Selassie, November 2.
- Grounation Day, April 21. Marks the day that Haile Selassie visited Jamaica in 1966.
- Ethiopian Constitution Day, July 16.
- Ethiopian New Year's Day, September 11.
- Rastafest. In 1982, the first international gathering of Rastafari groups occurred in Toronto, Canada. Since that time, an annual festival has taken place there as well as in other North American locations.

Common Misunderstandings, Stereotypes, and Classroom Concerns

African diaspora religions are not well understood in North America and are often dismissed as primitive and superstitious. It's common for African diaspora religions to be associated with Euro-American ideas of evil and the demonic. In the worst cases of stereotyping, these religions are linked with criminality. Naturally, with so many ways in which their religious lives may be misunderstood, many students exhibit considerable restraint in speaking about their religious lives. Students may identify as Christian even though African diaspora religions are mainly practiced in their households.

Ritually charged objects such as bracelets and amulets play protective roles in many African diaspora religions and some students may have such objects with them at school. Avoid touching all such sacred objects. If you wish to know more about an object that a student wears or brings to school, treat the object with respect. Only touch it with permission. Never try to remove a bracelet, necklace, or amulet as these items are worn for protective purposes and their removal could leave students feeling vulnerable. The head is considered a special zone where contact with sacred beings can happen. Be sure to ask permission before touching the head or the hair.

Don't expect that your students will be able to reveal a lot about their religions even if they wish to do so. It's common in African diaspora religions for non-initiates to receive help from diviners, healers, and other specialists without themselves being required to know a great deal about the religion's theological and cosmological underpinnings. Religions of the African diaspora are pragmatic religions that offer solutions to life's problems. They don't require the same level of knowledge and training for everyone. But there are some who come to know a great deal through initiatory processes. Respect the boundaries that initiatory religions place on what outsiders can know of the religion. If the student has received an initiation, there is much that he or she cannot reveal.

Students with extensive experience of African diaspora religions will likely excel in performative assignments, especially those that involve music. Experience with divination may yield the ability to discern patterns and formulate hypotheses based on observations of repeated patterns. Because many African diaspora communities tend toward collectivism, students with such backgrounds may be more comfortable with group work than some of their peers.

Further Reading and Resources

Atwood Mason, Michael. *Living Santería: Rituals and Experiences in an Afro-Cuban Religion.* Washington, DC: Smithsonian Books, 2002.

Barrett, Leonard E. *The Rastafarians: Sounds of Cultural Dissonance* (rev. and updated ed.). Boston: Beacon Press, 1988.

Brown, Karen McCarthy. *Mama Lola: A Vodou Priestess in Brooklyn* (updated and expanded ed.). Comparative Studies in Religion and Society: 4. Berkeley, CA: University of California Press, 2001.

Hepner, Randal L. "The House That Rasta Built: Church-Building and Fundamentalism among New York Rastafarians." In *Gatherings in Diaspora: Religious Communities and the New Immigration*. Edited by R. Stephen Warner and Judith G. Wittner, 197–234. Philadelphia, PA: Temple University Press, 1998.

Hernandez, Daisy. *A Cup of Water under My Bed: A Memoir*. Boston, MA: Beacon Press, 2014.

Maya, Deren. *Divine Horsemen: The Living Gods of Haiti*. London: Thames and Hudson, 1953.

Olmos, Margarite Fernández, Lizabeth Paravisini-Gebert, and Joseph Murphy, Foreword by Murphy. *Creole Religions of the Caribbean: An Introduction from Vodou and Santeria to Obeah and Espiritismo*. New York and London: NYU Press, 2011.

Richman, Karen E. *Migration and Vodou*. New World Diasporas. Gaineseville, FL: University Press of Florida, 2005.

What Is Rastafari? Tevya Heller, producer. Neighborhood: Los Angeles, CA: TMW Media Group, 2015.

Roberts, Donna C. and Donna Reed. *Yemanjá: Wisdom from the African Heart of Brazil*. Burlington, VT: Project Zula, 2015.

Voices of the Orishas. Directed by Alvaro Perez Betancourt.

3

Atheist, Agnostic, Humanist, and Anti-Religious Groups

In 2022, the Satanic Temple began renting space for an After School Satan Club at Donovan Elementary School, a public school in Lebanon, Ohio. Lebanon is a small rural town in southwestern Ohio. Like many public schools in rural America, Lebanon has an after-school religious club that is affiliated with Protestant Christianity. Due to a Supreme Court ruling in 2001 (Good News Club v. Milford Central School), public school districts in the United States cannot discriminate against religious, after-school groups that want to rent space. The Satanic Temple is a non-theistic religious group that offers alternative programming for students in public schools who, in the view of the Satanic Temple, are influenced by dominant religious groups such as Evangelical Protestant Christianity. Satanic Temple spokesperson, June Everett told Mawa Iqbal, an Ohio public radio reporter, that "we would prefer that the church, or any kind of church groups, stay completely out of the public sector. But since they're there, and we're allowed to be there, that's the reason we want to offer a safe place" (Iqbal). How did the Satanic Temple's after-school program originate in this rural town? Lebanon parents who were concerned about the oversized influence of a Christian after-school program called the Good News Club reached out to the Satanic Temple after their kids came home with permission slips to join the Christian club.

Introduction

This chapter offers guidance on the life-worlds and practices of students who have minimal or no religious affiliation. Educators should be aware that many homes in America are "religion-free zones" in the eyes of those who live there. By "religion-free," we mean free of organized religion, free of institutions that carry the label "religion." But humans are prone to asking about their place in the universe and the nature of reality and this existential stance cuts across the divide between religion and non-religion. The phrase "spiritual, but not religious" is frequently offered as a self-description by those who do not affiliate with any institutional form of religion. The Pew Research Center reported in 2024 that 28% of U.S. adults are religious "nones" – people who respond to the question of their religious identity by describing themselves as atheists, agnostics, or "nothing in particular." This data would suggest that nearly three out of every ten American homes are places where people identify as "spiritual, but not religious," atheist, or agnostic. Some of those non-religious homes have family members who do things that religious people typically do while ascribing to non-religion. They might, for example, belong to humanist organizations. They might associate with others who share their values and worldviews. They might even perform rituals affirming their commitment to a human-centered worldview. Educators need to understand the wide and vibrant range of options for contemporary students and families who reject conventional theism and the various stances that students and their families might take.

In this chapter, we define and discuss organized groups of people who question belief in God or divine beings. Atheism is a belief system that centers on a challenge to theism. Atheists claim that there are no deities. God doesn't exist. No other deities exist. Atheism is related to a skeptical attitude toward the question of divine beings: agnosticism. Agnostics say that they don't have enough evidence to make claims about the existence of God or other divine beings. They take the approach of reserving judgment on religious questions, leaving such discussions to others. Secular humanism is a system of thought and practice that centers humanity in ways that conventional religious groups center God or divine beings. For secular humanists, the solution to world problems will be found by looking to humans without seeking divine assistance. Secular humanist communities look to things like humanity's evolutionary success, the human capacity for imagination, our capacity for empathy, and the like as qualities that make humanity worthy of reverence. A related set of communities that focus on human beings but brand themselves as *religious* are groups that identify with religious humanism. Perhaps the most interesting stance covered in this chapter (associated with spectacular, media-friendly tactics and a high level of publicity) is represented by those groups who are organized along the lines of conventional religious groups but whose mission is anti-theistic. Exasperated by what they perceive as the hegemony of conservative Christianity in U.S. public life, anti-theistic and anti-religious groups are adept at using mockery to draw attention to their claims.

Anti-theistic religions such as the Satanic Temple decry the hegemony of Christianity in American public life, theatrically opposing the visible presence of Christianity in U.S. public life by offering tongue-in-cheek alternatives. What's good for the goose is good for the gander, the Satanic Temple says while erecting large statues of bare-chested, bearded, horned, pagan deities in town squares where the ten commandments have been put on display. Such anti-theistic groups tend to be informal in their organization and can be adhered to without visiting a sacred space such as a temple, mosque, or synagogue. Their tactics are sensational: they erect eye-catching statues of pre-Christian pagan deities that draw the public's attention to hypocrisy in the actions of state-empowered religious actors. Their horned deities stand as a reminder of pagan ways that existed prior to the rise of Christianity. But the horns of such statues also parody the idea that the courthouse is a place where the state should be erecting statues and tablets pronouncing moral codes. When Christians are perceived to be flexing their civil power in ways that the non-religious deem to be unconstitutional, members of the Satanic Temple flex their own. They erect stunning statues designed to make advocates of ten-commandment displays stop and consider whether it's worth the cost to share the stage with a horned pagan god.

Much that is philosophically non-religion presents itself sociologically as religion – one of the paradoxes that makes the study of non-religion so fascinating. Religious studies scholars, especially those who define religion as a social matter, tend to see religion operating in various social spheres, including secular spheres, of American public life. Religion is about social connections nurtured in spaces built for fellowship. Religion is not exclusively about God-talk or about the worship of deities. Many Americans who are "spiritual, but not religious," atheist, or agnostic assemble together in buildings, hold meetings that resemble religious services, offer values-based education to their children, collect funds for charitable projects, and otherwise engage in activities that resemble conventional organized religion. Being non-religious or anti-religious, if done with others in a consistent, institutional way, can be classified as a kind of devotion and therefore, arguably, as a kind of religion. In the mid-twentieth century, U.S. courts began to treat as legitimate the claims of non-theistic groups that they worship together and hence should be regarded as religions. For example, a California case in 1957 (Fellowship of Humanity v. Co. Alameda) settled the question of whether a non-theistic religious humanist group called the Fellowship of Humanity was entitled to a religious tax exemption. The courts who considered the Fellowship's arguments about their activities ruled that since the Fellowship of Humanity's buildings were being used for worship, the Fellowship should be considered a religion and exempt from paying taxes, just like more conventional organized religions.

Conscientious objectors in the twentieth century won legal protection from conscription for non-religious beliefs that war is unethical. Where legal recognition as religion was given to what humanist groups do because their organizational structure resembled more conventional religious groups, successful conscientious objectors established a new legal precedent: sincerity of belief. A key moment came in 1965, when the Supreme Court adopted a "parallel test" that defined as religious any "sincere and meaningful belief which occupies in the life of its possessor a place parallel to that filled by the God of those admittedly qualifying for the exemption" (United States v. Seeger, 380 U.S. 163, 176). Many of the plaintiffs in conscientious objector cases were young White men. They resembled their religious counterparts, such as Quaker, Mennonite, Catholic, and Jewish men, only they did not ground their objection to military service in their belief in God. Their cases show the government using the idea of sincerely held belief in a way that doesn't favor religion over non-religion. These cases also tell us much about how the benefits of religious freedom in the United States tend to be unevenly distributed based on who is asking to be recognized. From the 1940s to the 1970s, conscientious objector cases showed repeatedly that it's easier to be perceived as a sincere believer when you resemble other normatively religious people. Early twentieth-century women practicing Spiritualism were arrested for fortune-telling and denied the benefits of religious freedom.

Humanistic Groups

The Enlightenment philosophers of eighteenth-century Europe launched a number of movements that centered rationality and critiqued those elements of conventional religions that deviate from what they viewed as rational, such as the belief in miracles and reliance on the Bible as a source of revealed truth. One such movement that should be mentioned (although we won't dedicate space to it, given that it is not currently subscribed to by many students today) is deism, the belief that God created the world and then withdrew, leaving it to humanity to work out its situation. Many of the U.S. founding fathers were deists (such as Benjamin Franklin, Thomas Jefferson, and George Washington). The end of the nineteenth century and the beginning of the twentieth saw the rise of Darwinism and advances in Biblical criticism that undermined Christian and Jewish claims that Biblical scripture offers truth revealed by God. Instead of seeing the Bible as the infallible word of God, scholars in Biblical studies ushered in a view of the Bible as a resource to be used in many different ways.

Secular Humanism is the self-designation most common today for groups that center on humanity rather than the realm of the supernatural. Building on Enlightenment philosophy, figures like the French philosopher August Comte (1798–1857) were crucial to the development of secular humanism. Comte founded a Religion of Humanity in Paris. The Ethical Culture Movement was founded in 1876 by Felix Adler. It is a secular substitute for organized religion that emphasizes ethical conduct and social reform. Adler trained as a rabbi but left Judaism when he read the works of Kant and the neo-Kantian German philosopher Friedrich Albert Lange. Adler thought that traditional religions would eventually prove incompatible with a scientific worldview. Members of the movement commit to lifelong intellectual development. Adler emphasized ethics in the name of the movement since he felt that morality was a key aspect of religion that shouldn't disappear when conventional forms of organized religion fell by the wayside once rational. Ethical Culture Movement members devote any surplus income they have to the elevation of the working class. They aspire to sexual purity. The early twentieth century saw many institutional developments of secular humanism in America. The American Humanistic Association was founded in the 1920s. The philosopher John Dewey was a member of this organization, and he contributed to the composition of a Humanist Manifesto released by the organization in 1933. This Manifesto accounts for humanity as part of nature and eschews theistic explanations of the origin of the world and humanity. Many larger religious bodies include significant numbers of members and clergy who identify as being of humanist persuasion. Christian-generated humanistic groups are legion. A number of Unitarian Universalist ministers (see the Chapter on Unitarian Universalism in the Christianity section) contributed to the humanistic movement in the United States. The Quakers spawned a couple of groups. Non-theist Friends is a subgroup of the Religious Society of Friends (Quakers) that teaches a humanistic perspective. Another such Quaker-inspired group is The Humanist Society (formerly the Humanist Society of Friends).

Within Judaism, two groups can be classified as humanistic. The first group's moniker says it all: Humanistic Judaism. The second group, Reconstructionist Judaism, is open to theists and non-theists alike, placing its institutional efforts at making the human world a nurturing one.

There are so many secular uses of Buddhist meditation and other practices that garner calm and focus among Americans that adherents of secular Buddhism often outnumber religious Buddhists in smaller American towns. Only if a town or city has been settled by immigrant South Asians, Central Asians, Southeast Asians, or East Asians would it be easy to enter a holy sanctuary and chant a Buddhist liturgy with the requisite scents and sounds. Many small towns are full of bookstore Buddhists who might long for "the smells and bells" of religion, but have only books and gatherings of readers who buy books about Buddhism. Much the same came to be said of Hinduism, Jainism, and Sikhism, three other major South Asian religions. For historical reasons that need not detain us, there are fewer secular Hindus, secular Jains, and secular Sikhs than there are secular Buddhists. But they do exist and many of them attend the Hindu temple, the Jain shrine, or the Sikh gurdwara because that is where their friends gather. They go on Sundays to a place that is both a holy site and a mundane community center where the immigrant community gathers, speaks its languages, and perpetuates other customs from the motherland. Humanistic Buddhism includes groups like the Insight Meditation Movement. This modality of humanistic Buddhism combines the psychodynamic process of group therapy with more conventionally religious actions found in monastery-based Buddhist meditation retreats. This organization stresses mindfulness meditation. Its mindfulness meditation classes are popular in secular settings like city recreation centers and public schools as a non-religious way of focusing the mind. If a patient in a hospital wants to improve his or her mental state, she might join a mindfulness-based stress reduction program like that of Jon Kabat-Zinn.

Anti-Theistic and Atheistic Groups

The Satanic Temple is a Massachusetts-based religious organization that promotes rational thinking, common sense, and justice. This group does not worship Satan, but rather uses Satan as a metaphor to make fun of and subvert Christian dominance in American public culture. The Satanic Temple should not be confused with the Church of Satan, a theistic religious group that was founded by Anton Szandor LaVey in 1966. Church of Satan adherents worship Satan as a deity, using inversions of Catholic ceremonies such as the infamous Black Mass. While the Satanic Temple also uses the Black Mass ritual form, its adherents view Satan in a non-theistic way. For the Satanic Temple, Satan stands for how humans should wisely relate to claims of divine power. For them, Satan is a symbol of rational rebellion and not a deity as such. Satanic Temple adherents draw on images of spiritual rebellion found in Gnostic Christian writings. Gnostic literature, common in the first centuries of Christianity before Gnosticism was declared heretical, stresses rebellion against false claims of deity. According to Gnostic Gospels, the first humans achieved wisdom by rebelling against a jealous demigod being who falsely proclaimed himself God. Like the first humans, Satan also rebels against one who declares himself God. Satan personifies wise rebellion. Satan is, furthermore, a fierce-looking figure who shows his great power by the vast number of minions he has at his disposal. Hence Satan serves well as a symbol of what the Satanic Temple values: a spirit of rebellion and means of empowerment against the dominion of conservative Christians in America.

The Satanic Temple began in 2013, founded by Lucian Greaves and Malcolm Jarry. The organization originally had a principled stance of not pursuing tax exemption while otherwise operating as a religious organization. But this changed in 2019 when then-President Donald Trump signed an executive order that weakened a provision of the U.S. tax code that prohibits non-profit groups from endorsing or opposing political candidates. The Temple applied for and gained tax-exempt status from the Internal Revenue Service at that time.

The Satanic Temple uses serious parody to counter what they regard as undue influence of Christian groups in American public spaces. They entered the limelight in 2013 by staging a mock rally in support of Republican Florida governor Rick Scott, who had signed a bill allowing students to deliver "inspirational messages" at public school events, effectively allowing prayer meetings to be conducted during school hours. Satanic Temple members at the rally chanted "Hail Satan, Hail Rick Scott" and showed visible enthusiasm for the bill.

In 2016, the Temple began offering After School Satan Clubs in response to the Evangelical Christian "Good News Clubs" that sprung up across the country after the favorable U.S. Supreme Court judgment of 2001. When the Satanic Temple becomes aware of clubs organized by the Child Evangelism Fellowship, the organization that offers Good News Clubs in American public schools, they offer alternate after-school programs. Good News Clubs have been operating in public schools since the 1940s, offering after-school activities that teach a literal interpretation of the Bible. There are over 3,500 Good News Clubs operating in public schools today. The Satanic Temple uses its own after-school programming to give children an alternative and to draw attention to what they regard as the establishment of Christianity as a state religion. Citing Constitutional language that prohibits the government from promoting one religion above another, the Satanic Temple offers educators information on alternative programs on its website. In certain states where not legally prohibited, the Satanic Temple offers the *Satanic Children's Big Book of Activities*. This collection of cartoons, word scrambles, and other educational activities was originally distributed in Orange County, Florida public schools after a court ruling made it legal to disseminate Bibles there.

The Church of the Flying Spaghetti Monster, also known as the Pastafarians, is a group whose methods align closely with those of the Satanic Temple. Founded in 2005 by a college graduate with a B.S. in physics, the Pastafarians use absurdity to score rhetorical points. They take pasta as their object of worship and pose for social media photos and protest meetings wearing pasta strainers on their heads. Popular among some college students and those who identify as free-thinkers and atheists, the Pastafarians have many of the marks of organized religion. They congregate regularly at protest meetings and at their annual conference. They have a shared body of symbols and practices. Like the Satanic Temple, this parodic group knows how to score points and make an impression on the public. They use serious satire to achieve their goal of eliminating what they regard as special protections and privileges for religious people.

Many Pastafarians identify as atheists and adhere to the New Atheist movement, founded by Richard Dawkins and Sam Harris. New atheists wish to see the decline of religion. They say religious truth claims are untrue and associate a rational world with a religion-free world.

Eclectic Groups

While not numerically a large group, the Church of Body Modification should be mentioned: it is an important group for educators to know about. Members of the Church honor the body as a site for spiritual practice. The group has around 3,500 members and does work to support the creation of a vital spiritual bond between body, mind, and soul. Members of the Church of Body Modification engage in practices like piercing, tattooing, scarification, fire-walking, and the like. The Church of Body Modification has had legal success in school settings, including a 2010 case in which the American Civil Liberties Union defended a 14-year-old member of the Church who had been suspended from a North Carolina public school for wearing a nose stud. A federal judge ruled in favor of the girl's right to wear a nose stud.

Groups that practice tattooing as a religious practice have been successful in obtaining legal redress from employers with dress codes that prohibit body modifications. This is the case of a Red Robin employee with wrist tattoos in Coptic (an ancient Egyptian language) expressing his devotion to Ra, the Sun God, as part of the Kemetic religion, an ancient Egyptian religious group. The employee was fired from a restaurant in Seattle that had a policy against visible tattoos. In 2005, the employee won the right to have his religious practice accommodated by his employer. Title VII requires employers to make reasonable accommodations for sincerely held religious beliefs to accommodate those beliefs will cause undue hardship to the business. Red Robin argued that any exceptions to its dress code policy would damage the wholesome image that the restaurant chain cultivates. The court was not persuaded by this argument.

Common Misunderstandings and Stereotypes

Educators should be aware of the wide range of stances and goals within non-religious or anti-religious groups. Some eschew the label "religion" while others seek out the label "religion," only to wear like it (like the Satanic Temple), as a satirical party hat that mocks what is most sacred to many Christians, especially those at the conservative end of the Christian spectrum. Some groups just want to disprove the truth claims of theists; they have no political or legal agenda. Others want to eradicate all religion from public life; they support political and legal initiatives to do just that. Others want to carry the label "theist" into new spheres, perhaps ecological or scientific. Some groups, like the Satanic Temple, have a political mission. Others are more *laissez faire*. They simply want nothing to do with religion personally. Like a teetotaler at a boozy party, they often don't mind if others partake of religious life in their presence.

The most pernicious stereotype that affects all such groups is the perception that they all uniformly oppose the practice of religion. Groups that adhere to non-religion in the United States are an incredibly diverse patchwork quilt of groups. Some, it is true, wish to see the practice of religion banished from public life. While it's safe to say that most atheists oppose religion, not all do. Many non-religious groups don't wish to prevent people from practicing their religion. Rather, they want to see religion play a smaller role in American public spaces, especially public spheres supported by tax dollars. Many simply want to see conservative Evangelical Christian religion play a less dominant role in American public life.

It's commonplace for atheist, agnostic, and non-religious groups to be seen as immoral. In fact, the considered stance of groups such as secular humanists or the Ethical Culture Movement makes them morally sensitive thinkers who may well be more concerned with the welfare of their fellow humans than some conventionally religious people. Even the controversial Satanic Temple group cannot be condemned as lacking morals. It is a concern for the well-being of their fellow citizens whose rights are being trampled that compels members of their group to court outrage with publicity stunts that draw attention to their cause.

Culturally Responsive Pedagogy

Many young people find religion fascinating. Likewise, opposition to religion abounds in young people. These are topics that often provoke real passion. New atheists, in particular, are notorious for their firebrand intensity. Such passion can be contagious, leading to some powerful discussions. Some of the emotionality that discussion of religion and non-religion induces can be used when teaching about a topic that should be approached with real feeling. Perhaps you'd like to engage the class on a topic like the legality of abortion or medically assisted death, topics that have grave consequences for how we live our lives. With such topics, it's critical that students engage rather than remain apathetic and uninterested. Approaching these topics through the lens of religion and non-religion might be useful as a way to generate strong feelings.

Debate is a logical way to play to the strengths of students who take pride in atheist, agnostic, and anti-religious stances and subcultures. Organizing debates that require such students to consider the premises held by their counterparts "across the aisle" can maximize opportunities for learning. Another activity might be to group non-believers with those who identify as religious and task groups with creating an exhibit or narrative that shows religion in conversation with non-religion or anti-religion.

Further Reading and Resources

Child Evangelism Fellowship website. https://www.cefonline.com
Church of the Flying Spaghetti Monster website. https://www.spaghettimonster.org/about/
Church of Satan website. https://www.churchofsatan.com/
Cascone, Sarah. "Satanic Coloring Books Distributed at Florida Public Schools." *Art World*, September 17, 2014. https://news.artnet.com/art-world/satanic-coloring-books-distributed-at-florida-public-schools-105119
Dubler, Joshua, and Isaac Weiner, eds. *Religion, Law, USA*. New York: NYU Press, 2019.
Fellowship of Humanity v. Co. Alameda. https://law.justia.com/cases/california/court-of-appeal/2d/153/673.html
Good News Club v. Milford Central School. https://www.oyez.org/cases/2000/99-2036
Hail Satan. 2019 documentary directed by Penny Lane.
I, Pastafari: A Flying Spaghetti Monster Story. A 2020 documentary directed by Michael Arthur.
Iqbal, Mawa. "Lebanon Elementary School to Host after School Satan Club." WYSO.org, January 28, 2022. https://www.wyso.org/local-and-statewide-news/2022-01-28/lebanon-elementary-school-to-host-after-school-satan-club
Kaiser, Lydia. "Is There a Satan Club in Your Child's School?" Child Evangelism Fellowship website, May 2, 2022. https://www.cefonline.com/articles/teach-kids-articles/is-there-a-satan-club-in-your-childs-school/
Laycock, Joseph. *Speak of the Devil: How The Satanic Temple Is Changing the Way We Talk about Religion*. New York: Oxford University Press, 2020.
Laycock, Joseph. "Austrian Court Okays Head-Colander in Driver's License: Is Pastafarianism Becoming a Religion?" *Religion Dispatches*, July 18, 2011.
McCrary, Charles. "Fortune Telling and American Religious Freedom." *Religion & American Culture* 28, no. 2 (Summer, 2018): 269–306.
McCrary, Charles. "Secularism, Pluralism, and Publics in America." In *The Oxford Research Encyclopedia of Religion in America*, ed. John Corrigan. New York: Oxford University Press, 2018.

Netter, Sarah. "Student's Body Modification Religion Questioned after Nose Piercing Controversy." *ABC News*, September 15, 2010. https://abcnews.go.com/us/students-body-modification-religion-questioned-nose-piercing-controversy/story?id=11645847

Niose, David. *Nonbeliever Nation: The Rise of Secular Americans*. London: Palgrave Macmillan, 2012.

Russo, Charles J. "How After-School Clubs Became a New Battleground in the Satanic Temple's Push to Preserve Separation of Church and State." *The Conversation*, July 21, 2023.

Satanic Temple website. https://thesatanictemple.com/

Schmidt, Leigh Eric. *The Church of Thomas Paine: A Religious History of American Secularism*. Princeton, NJ: Princeton University Press, 2023.

Schmidt, Leigh Eric. *Village Atheists: How America's Unbelievers Made Their Way in a Godly Nation*. Princeton, NJ: Princeton University Press, 2019.

Seales, Rebecca. "The Satanic Temple: Think You Know about Satanists? Maybe You Don't." *BBC News*, May 20, 2023. https://www.bbc.com/news/world-us-canada-65549975

Smith, Gregory A. "About Three in Ten U.S. Adults Are Now Religiously Unaffiliated." Pew Research Center, December 14, 2021. https://www.pewresearch.org/religion/2021/12/14/about-three-in-ten-u-s-adults-are-now-religiously-unaffiliated/

Weiner, Isaac. "The Sabbath Observer, The Idiosyncratist, and the Religious Organization: How the EEOC Imagines Religion at Work." *Religion & American Culture* 32, no. 3 (Fall 2023): 305–37. doi:10.1017/rac.2022.12.

United States v. Seeger, 380 U.S. 163 (1965). https://www.oyez.org/cases/1964/50

4

Baha'i

> On a summer day in Chicago, a Baha'i teenager joins her friends (Baha'i and non-Baha'i) on a bike tour that is both educational and activist in nature. During a two-hour cycling tour, she will learn about how an unjust racist killing sparked the Chicago Race Riot of 1919 that came to be known as the Red Summer. This teenager takes a keen interest in social justice; her religion teaches that to be pious is to fight racism.

Introduction

It's estimated that there are some 7 million Baha'is in the world, with adherents in every country.[1] India has the largest population of Baha'is in the world. The United States has the second largest population. Chicago is the site of one of the first Baha'i communities to be established in America. The only Baha'i temple in North America is located in Wilmette, a suburb north of Chicago. Over 250,000 people, both Baha'i and non-Baha'i, visit this temple each year.

Historical Overview

The religion began in Persia (now Iran) in the nineteenth century. One key figure in the early history is a young man (the Bab) who preached the imminent birth of a prophet and was put to death as a heretic by state authorities loyal to Islam. The Bab's tomb is located in Haifa, Israel. It's an important place of pilgrimage for Baha'is. Another figure is a man named Baha'u'llah who claimed to be the awaited prophet. Certain descendants of Baha'u'llah also play a prominent role in the religion. All these key figures experienced persecution, including exile and imprisonment.

Baha'is assert the unity of all religions, describing how God's divine will has been revealed through the major religions of the world. These revelations take the form of separate dispensations, each offering a more advanced revelation than the last. Baha'is work to create "a unified world" inclusive of all humanity. God has created all humans as equals. Women and men are said to be the two wings that enable the bird of humanity to soar. People should treat each other with empathy and consideration so as to ensure the oneness of humanity, regardless of national borders. Poverty should be eliminated, along with the class divides that prevent humans from identifying with each other.

Baha'is over the age of 15 are required to recite daily prayers. Adult Baha'is observe a daytime fast for 19 days in March. Tithing is expected. Alcohol consumption is forbidden. Baha'is are not to engage in gossip; even partisan politics are problematic in light of the unity of humanity. Baha'is practice their religion while doing useful work. Monasticism is not permitted. Baha'is should not rely on begging for their sustenance. Sexuality is restricted to married men and women: premarital, extramarital, and same-sex sexuality are not permitted.

The organizational structure of the Baha'i religion centers on laypeople: there are no clergy. Laypeople serve in the elected bodies that govern Baha'is life. Although men are in theory accorded no special status in the religion, it is only men that serve in the Universal House of Justice, the central governing body of the religion.

Holidays

- The Baha'i New Year corresponds to the traditional Iranian New Year and is celebrated on the spring equinox.
- 19-Day Fast. This fast precedes the New Year. Baha'is from ages 15–70 fast from sunrise to sunset for a 19-day period in March. Those who are ill, who do heavy labor, who are pregnant, nursing, or menstruating are exempt from the obligation to fast.
- The Birth of the Bab, celebrated on the first day of the eighth new moon following the Baha'i New Year, a date that fluctuates from mid-October to mid-November in the Gregorian calendar.
- The Birth of Baha'u'llah, celebrated on the day after the birth of the Bab celebration.
- 19-Day Feasts are regular community gatherings that occur once every Baha'i month. The Baha'i year consists of 19 months, each having 19 days.

Common Misunderstandings, Stereotypes, and Classroom Concerns

Because the religion originated in a Muslim-majority country and many Baha'is in the United States follow Iranian customs such as celebrating the Iranian New Year, sometimes Baha'is are assumed to be Muslims. But it is quite likely that people simply know nothing of the religion. If that's the case, some may use the typical put-downs associated with lesser-known religions or new religious movements: "you belong to a cult," "you've been brain-washed," etc.

For Baha'i children, age 15 and over, care should be taken with requiring strenuous athletics during the month of March.

Those who are not exempt from the obligation to fast take no food or drink from sunrise to sunset for a 19-day period in March. Another concern when it comes to athletics is the high value placed on modesty in this religion. Children should be allowed to keep their body covered.

Prayers should be accommodated during school hours. Of the three prayers that Baha'is are to observe each day, two occur during the school day. There is a brief prayer that is to be recited between noon and sunset. There is also a thrice-daily prayer (repeated morning, noon, and evening) that is likely to be performed at noon on school days. The student will need washing facilities to purify hands and face prior to the noon prayer; for the prayer itself, the student will need a space where bending and sitting are possible.

Baha'is work very hard to develop empathy and treat others fairly, so Baha'i students will likely flourish when group work is assigned. The religion's central belief in the equality of all humans regardless of class, race, gender, nationality, or religion makes it likely that your Baha'i students will excel at work that is geared toward social justice.

Note

1   Langness, David, "How Many Baha'is?," *Bahai Teachings.Org*. October 2, 2013.

Further Reading and Resources

Bahá'u'lláh, 'Alī Muḥammad Shīrāzī Bāb, and 'Abdu'l-Bahá. *Baha'i Prayers; a Selection of the Prayers Revealed by Bahá'u'lláh, The Báb, and 'Abdu'l-Bahá*. Chicago: Baha'i Pub. Committee, 1969.
Hartz, Paula. *Baha'i Faith*. New York: Infobase Publishing, 2009.
McMullen, Michael. *The Baha'i: The Religious Construction of a Global Identity*. New Brunswick, NJ: Rutgers University Press, 2000.
Stockman, Robert H. *The Baha'i Faith in America*. Chicago: Baha'i Pub. Trust, 1985.

5

Buddhism

> In Myanmar, the residents of a village gather as monks in saffron-colored robes and shave the head of a young man as he is ordained to join their order, chanting that he takes refuge in "the Buddha, the Dharma, and the Sangha." Thousands of miles away in Japan, a small crowd stands before a giant statue of another Buddha named Amida, praying to him in hopes that they will be reborn in his heavenly "Pure Land." Meanwhile, in northern India among scattered members of diaspora Tibetan communities, flags printed with scriptural passages fly in the wind, in the hope that their messages will be carried off into the cosmos. And continents away in a makeshift temple in Chicago, people gather on mats to sit quietly in mindful meditation on their breathing, aiming to still the turnings of their mind. Though distinct in geography, form, and purpose, each of these groups is taking part in practices rooted in and central to the diversity of ancient Buddhist traditions.

Introduction

According to various estimates, there are approximately 500 million Buddhists in the world.[1]

It is the majority religion in the countries of Southeast Asia (Cambodia, Myanmar, Thailand, Sri Lanka, and Vietnam) and has had a lasting cultural impact in Nepal, China, Japan, and

India, the land of its birth. Additionally, some three to four million Buddhists live in the United States, the majority of whom are Asian American. Across its history, Buddhist traditions have generated lasting contributions to the fields of literature, art, psychology, philosophy, and, more recently, popular culture. Its scriptures and texts have been written in Pali, Sanskrit, Chinese, Tibetan, Japanese, and scores of other local languages. As this diversity suggests, there are many different schools of Buddhist thought which often take very different positions from one another. In this chapter, we will provide an overview of the historical development and key ideas of these Buddhist traditions, cover some of their main scriptures and festivals, and finally discuss several common misconceptions that may have an impact on the classroom.

Historical Overview

Buddhist traditions trace themselves back to an individual named Siddhartha Gautama, sometimes also referred to as Shakyamuni ("Sage of the Shakyas"). While little historical data exists about Gautama's life beyond the multiple legends that have been passed down, it is thought that he lived in what is now modern-day Nepal between the fifth to sixth centuries before the Common Era, with the unverified dates sometimes given of 563–483 BCE. According to popular stories, Gautama was a prince of the Shakya clan, but abandoned his royal upbringing to pursue religious insight. In these stories, it is often said that after living in opulence and pleasure for most of his life, where unpleasant scenes were kept from him, the prince was inspired to leave his royal environment by witnessing the Four Sights: an elderly person, a sick person, a corpse, and then a monk who had left behind all worldly possessions to seek spiritual truth. Gautama is said to have abandoned the palace and, after years of arduous training and effort, achieved a state referred to as nirvana (literally, "to blow out" or "extinguish") and took the title Buddha, which translates literally to "Awakened One." As this phrase suggests, Buddhist traditions believe that a Buddha's understanding and outlook separate such a person from other individuals in the same way wakefulness is distinct from unconsciousness. A Buddha is thought to possess an entirely different level of awareness from other beings. Within all Buddhist traditions there are thought to be multiple Buddhas, either one after another historically or simultaneously, and Siddhartha Gautama holds special importance as the Buddha of this particular world age who reinvigorated the Buddhist teaching.

After achieving nirvana, Gautama Buddha is said to have begun spreading that teaching, referred to as dharma. "Dharma" can be translated in a variety of ways, for instance as simply "teaching" or even "law." The latter sense conveys the notion that, from the Buddhist point of view, the elements of the Buddha's teaching are timeless truths woven into the nature of life, perhaps akin to the laws of physics. In their simplest form, the teachings are conveyed in what is called the Four Noble Truths, enumerated as follows, with descriptions.

1. *Life is characterized by suffering, pain, and dissatisfaction.* As Buddhists frequently explain, this statement does not mean to say that there are no good things about life, but rather to admit the fact that pleasures do not last forever and sickness, old age, and death are universal and unavoidable. In other words, people want good experiences to last forever and to always avoid bad experiences, which is simply impossible.
2. *The cause of suffering, pain, and dissatisfaction is desire.* Our unreasonable desire to cling to pleasure and completely avoid suffering increases dissatisfaction as both goals are impossible. As craving and desire are insatiable, they are sometimes referred to as a kind of fire or thirst in Buddhist teachings. In many early Buddhist texts, one common source of craving and desire is each individual's sense of self. Whereas people do not want themselves to change (such as by growing older or losing their health), Buddhist precepts hold that a sense of a permanent self is an illusion as all things are temporary and constantly undergoing change.

3. *Nirvana is a state where this unreasonable desire ceases to exist.* Nirvana's literal meaning of "to blow out" or "extinguish" applies in this sense to the fire or thirst of desire, and its state of peace and equanimity is offered as the solution to the problems stated above.
4. *Nirvana can be achieved by following the Eightfold Path.* The Eightfold Path, as a method by which to achieve the stillness of mind where unreasonable desires cease, is a series of ethical and meditative practices made up of the following elements: Right Understanding, Right Thought, Right Speech, Right Action, Right Livelihood, Right Effort, Right Mindfulness, and Right Concentration. These practices are sometimes grouped into three categories of Morality, Meditation, and Wisdom.

Beyond freeing a person from desire and suffering, from the Buddhist point of view achieving nirvana also ends one's repeated rounds of death and rebirth. Like other religions of India, the Buddhist worldview holds that existence is composed of a cycle of death and rebirth. Based on their karma, or the actions they have committed during life, a being is reborn in either a higher state (such as a celestial figure or a human) or in a lower one (such as an animal or in a hell). A Buddha or other awakened being is thought to have extinguished his or her karma and escaped this round of endless death and rebirth.

To spread these teachings, soon after his awakening Gautama Buddha is said to have founded the first Buddhist sangha, or community. Some members of the community became ordained as monks or (later on) nuns who gave up family, households, and material possessions to live in monasteries and temples. Other members of the community remained householders and supported the monasteries through donations of food and other necessary items. Together, the three elements of Buddha (the founder), dharma (the teaching), and sangha (community) are sometimes referred to as the Three Jewels, forming the foundation of the Buddhist way of life.

As time went on and Buddhism spread, different teachings and ways of thought began to appear. One especially important movement, eventually called Mahayana ("Great Vehicle"), deemphasized the distinction between monks and laypeople and otherwise reinterpreted aspects of the preceding teachings. For example, Mahayana Buddhist schools of thought put forward what is known as the bodhisattva ("awakened being") path, a perspective that argues for all individuals to pursue awakening just like Gautama Buddha. The Mahayana also emphasized certain philosophical concepts, such as "emptiness," the belief that all things are interdependent, interrelated, and thus closely interconnected, meaning that all beings are part of a universal "Buddha-nature." Due to the teachings of the bodhisattva path and a universal Buddha-nature, the Mahayana sees the universe as filled with multiple Buddhas and awakened beings besides Gautama Buddha. From the beginning, this Mahayana way of thought was most likely an umbrella term for many different kinds of Buddhist schools and over time these groups continued to subdivide.

While the Buddhist presence in India decreased, these different schools took root across Asia. The Mahayana forms of Buddhism became the dominant kind in China, Japan, and Tibet. In China and Japan, two important schools formed within Mahayana Buddhism. The first is Pure Land Buddhism, which focuses on chanting and ritual activity aimed at resulting in a rebirth in realms created by celestial Buddhas and bodhisattvas. The Zen ("meditation") school stresses meditations and rituals meant to achieve insight, either suddenly or gradually, into one's own inherent Buddha-nature. Tibetan Buddhism, sometimes also called Vajrayana ("Thunderbolt Vehicle" or "Diamond Vehicle"), developed an elaborate system of clergy and teachers known as lamas, of whom the Dalai Lama is a leading member. Tibetan or Vajrayana Buddhism is distinguished by rituals, chants, and visualization exercises employing one's own body or physical form as a pathway to insight and awakening. In Southeast Asia, a school known as Theravada ("Way of the Elders") became the primary form of Buddhism. Theravada Buddhism is distinct from Mahayana Buddhism by largely still holding to the distinction between monks and laypeople, not emphasizing the bodhisattva path, and focusing primarily on the life and teachings of Gautama Buddha, as opposed to other awakened beings. Either through Asian immigrant communities or converts, all these Buddhist schools are present in many parts of the world, including the United States.

Scriptures and Festivals

There are many important Buddhist scriptures. The following is only a partial list, given alphabetically.

- *Buddhacarita* – A poetic rendering of the story of Siddhartha Gautama's journey to become the Buddha.
- *Dhammapada* – An early collection of sayings attributed to Gautama Buddha.
- *Heart Sutra* – A popular Mahayana text; it explores the concept of "emptiness" explained above.
- *Jatakamala* – An enormous collection of tales of Gautama Buddha's past lives.
- *Lotus Sutra* – A key Mahayana text, influential especially for the later Chinese and Japanese schools.
- *The Platform Sutra of the Sixth Patriarch* – This Chinese text provides some of the foundation for the "Zen" school.
- *Tripitaka* – Meaning "Triple Basket," this collection is written in the Pali language and is composed of the *Nikayas* (texts and teachings), *Vinaya* (monastic regulations), and *Abhidharma* (philosophical treatises).
- *Sukhavativyuha Sutra (Infinite Life Sutra)* – An influential text in the Pure Land tradition.
- *Vimalakirti Sutra* – A popular Mahayana text that emphasizes the bodhisattva path for householders and the concept of emptiness.

Similarly, there are many different Buddhist festivals, many of which are particular to a country or region. Rather than attempt to list them all, instead the following are examples of festivals celebrated by most Buddhists and a few highlights of celebrations particular to some Buddhist cultural regions or communities.

- *Vesak* – Named after the month of Vesakha, this holiday celebrates the birth, awakening, and death of Gautama Buddha. Usually it occurs in April, May, or June, depending on the lunar calendar. Celebrants may chant texts, bathe statues of the Buddha, or engage in other commemorations of his life.
- *Bodhi Day* – Occurring in December, this festival highlights Siddhartha Gautama's achievement of awakening. Observing Buddhists may celebrate this event through offerings, chanting, or festival meals.
- *Magha Puja* (also called "Sangha Day") – Celebrated throughout Southeast Asia, this event commemorates a gathering between the Buddha and a number of his first followers. Those observing the festival make offerings to the local temple and attend teachings offered by ordained Buddhists.
- *Hungry Ghost Festival* – Primarily a Chinese Buddhist ceremony, on the fifteenth day of the seventh month of the Chinese lunar calendar, celebrants make offerings to dead relatives to assist their auspicious rebirths.

Common Misunderstandings, Stereotypes, and Classroom Concerns

Asian American students are stereotypically believed to be "smart" and "good at math." These stereotypes are described well by the "model minority myth," the idea that Asians as a group are highly intelligent, diligent, hardworking overachievers. As Alice Li explains in a TEDx talk, the model minority myth leads to fewer Asian Americans filing discrimination claims because they feel they would not be believed. The model minority myth proclaims that race is irrelevant to success in America: "just look at the Asians." By the same token, Asian American students often feel disinclined to speak up about racism they experience. The model minority myth suggests that Asian students will always succeed; they will be rewarded for their diligence and innate intelligence. In addition, the model minority myth exacerbates the divide between Asian Americans and other minorities, leading to Asian American students feeling isolated from other students of color who experience racism. The "perpetual foreigner syndrome" that stems from the underrepresentation of Asians in Western media has similar ramifications for Asian American students. It contributes to isolation. When educators assume that Asian American students are outsiders with a limited ability to fit into American institutions who nonetheless will thrive due to their work ethic and prodigious intellectual gifts, the "model minority myth" and "the perpetual foreigner syndrome" will lead many Buddhist students to feel isolated from peers and school personnel.

There are several other misunderstandings and stereotypes to be watchful for when dealing with Buddhist students. The first is to avoid certain generalizations. For instance, despite its importance in Buddhist tradition, not all Buddhists meditate nor do all Buddhists see the practice of "mindfulness" (conscious awareness of actions and surroundings) as the central tenet of the religion. Similarly, though non-violence is a value held by many Buddhists, not all Buddhists are vegan or vegetarian. Many do avoid eating meat and animal products and those who make offerings to monks or nuns prefer to do so with vegetarian items. However, due to the wide array of countries from which Buddhists come, it is not safe to assume that all Buddhists are vegan or vegetarian. On a related note, it is also not safe to assume that all Buddhists are committed pacifists. Several historical examples exist of Buddhist involvement in violent acts, from the Zen nationalism of Imperial Japan in World War II to the current aggression against Rohingya Muslim minorities in Myanmar.

Other frequent misunderstandings involve taking one part of Buddhist tradition and interpreting it as holding for the entire religion. For example, due to the emphasis in some Buddhist schools on philosophical exploration, a generalization has emerged that Buddhism is more a philosophy than a religion. The original term "dharma," which many Buddhists use rather than "Buddhism" to refer to their practices, encompasses philosophy, religion, and even psychology. As many Buddhists around the world participate in rituals, festivals, believe in various supernatural beings, and have a complicated metaphysical worldview, Buddhism should be considered both a philosophy and a religion. Other examples include attributing the concept of Zen to all of Buddhism, when in fact it is just one school within the larger umbrella of Buddhism. Similarly, perhaps due to intense media presence since the Chinese invasion of Tibet in the mid-twentieth century, the Dalai Lama has at times been regarded as a representative of all Buddhists, whereas in actual fact he only holds most importance for some select subgroups of Tibetan Buddhism. Finally, images of *Budai* (the so-called "Laughing Buddha" or "Fat Buddha"), a popular East Asian form of a particular awakened being named *Maitreya*, are often wrongly taken as depictions of Gautama Buddha or seen as an emblematic of all Buddhas.

One final caution should be given regarding the classroom use of mindfulness, meditation, or other Buddhist practices. At times, instructors have seen fit to use these elements in the classroom, either in lessons on Buddhism or simply as relaxation exercises. In doing so, one should be careful to avoid cultural appropriation as well as the appearance of advancing religious practice. While mindfulness, perhaps somewhat like yoga (which also has a religious background), in popular usage has been detached from its religious context, teachers should be aware of that context and the position in which it places students who might object to the practice due to their own conflicting personal beliefs.

Culturally Responsive Pedagogy

A teacher with Buddhist students in the classroom can take several steps to ensure a culturally responsive environment. First, instructors can make certain that the cultural background of Buddhist students is present in the classroom. For example, in discussions of history, one can be sure to highlight the contributions of Buddhism across Asia, where the tradition has influenced dynasties and political movements in India, China, Japan, Mongolia, and across Southeast Asia. In the field of art, one could highlight the massive statues of Buddhas in central Asia, the potential interactions between Buddhist and Greek sculptors, or the intricacies of tantric mandalas as instances of Buddhist achievement in art. In literature, where discussions often focus on Western works such as Homer's *Iliad* or Dante's *Divine Comedy*, one could include *Buddhacarita*, a poetic imagination of the life of Siddhartha Gautama's journey to Buddhahood by the ancient Indian author Ashvaghosha, or *Journey to the West* by Wu Cheng'en, a classic sixteenth-century Chinese novel that blends Buddhist thought with Confucian and Daoist principles.

A second strategy for culturally responsive pedagogy with Buddhist students is to draw from their prior knowledge and experience, while being careful to make certain individuals do not feel pressured to share. In the case of Buddhist students, those who do meditate or practice mindfulness, they could describe or discuss those customs with their peers. Assignments or presentations could also be crafted in such a way that Buddhist students could connect them to their traditions and share their experiences in the ways most comfortable to them. Inclusion of Buddhist ideas, texts, history, and the experiences of individual students in these kinds of ways could serve to help better incorporate Buddhist students or students from a Buddhist background into the classroom.

Note

1 These and other population estimates in this chapter are drawn from research done by the Pew Research Center. "The Global Religious Landscape," December 18, 2012, https://www.pewresearch.org/religion/2012/12/18/global-religious-landscape-exec/#:~:text=The%20demographic%20study%20%E2%80%93%20based%20on,the%20world%20as%20of%202010.

Further Reading and Resources

Gethin, Rupert. *The Foundations of Buddhism*. New York: Oxford University Press, 1998.

Gombrich, Richard. *Theravada Buddhism: A Social History from Ancient Benares to Modern Colombo*. New York: Routledge, 1988.

Harvey, Peter. *An Introduction to Buddhism*. Cambridge: Cambridge University Press, 2012.
Li, Alice. "Why Asian Americans Are Not the Model Minority." TEDx Talks. Vanderbilt University. https://www.youtube.com/watch?v=87QkjfUEbz4
Lopez, Donald, Jr., ed. *Buddhist Scriptures*. Edited by Donald S. Lopez, Jr. New York: Penguin Press, 2004.
Lopez, Donald, Jr., ed. *Buddhism in Practice*. Princeton, NJ: Princeton University Press, 1998.
In the Buddha's Words: An Anthology of Discourses from the Pali Canon. Translated by Bhikkhu Bodhi. Boston, MA: Shambhala Press, 2005.
Powers, John. *Introduction to Tibetan Buddhism*. Ithaca, NY: Snow Lion Publications, 1995.
Rahula, Walpola. *What the Buddha Taught*. New York: Grove Press, 1974.
Sayings of the Buddha: A Translation of the Dhammapada. Translated by Rupert Gethin. New York: Oxford University Press, 2008.
Seager, Richard. *Buddhism in America*. New York: Columbia University Press, 1999.
Strong, John. *The Buddha: A Short Biography*. Oxford: Oneworld Press, 2001.
Tanahashi, Kazuaki, and Peter Levitt, eds. *The Essential Dogen: Writings of the Great Zen Master*. Boston, MA: Shambhala Press, 2013.
Williams, Paul. *Mahayana Buddhism*. New York: Routledge Press, 1989.

6

Chinese Religions: Falun Gong

In a city park in upstate New York, a crowd gathers, engaging in breathing, meditation, and stretching exercises, their movements fluid and unified. At the same time, elsewhere in the world, in the streets of cities such as Toronto or Los Angeles, protesters march, carrying banners that decry the treatment of prisoners in China, attempting to call attention to what they see as inhumane detention for those wishing to openly practice their beliefs. Meanwhile, in a practitioner's home, a small group meets to discuss the writings of Li Hongzhi, considering the ways in which they can advance their practices according to the descriptions laid out in those texts.

Introduction

Falun Gong, sometimes also called "Falun Dafa," translates roughly to "Great Law Wheel" and was founded in China in the early 1990s by Li Hongzhi. After the movement was banned in China in 1999, it spread worldwide and, according to some estimates (although numbers are difficult to confirm given the group's loose organization structure), may have as many as 20 million followers today. Given this tension with the land of its birth, an ongoing theme of contemporary Falun Gong is non-violent protest against the government of China. The main headquarters of the movement now rests in upstate New York in the United States. Though members of the movement frequently identify it strictly as a moral philosophy, as we will see, there are many connections between Falun Gong and other religious traditions, justifying its inclusion in a volume of this kind. In the following, we will delve into the historical background of the movement, some of its key tenets and practices, and ways instructors can reach out to Falun Gong members in their classrooms.

Historical Overview

Li Hongzhi began publishing his articulation of practices, which he called "Falun Gong," with the intention of leading individuals to greater health and spiritual insight in 1992, then began lecturing across China and other countries in the mid-1990s. Central to his teachings, he argued, were the concepts of ren (benevolence), zhen (truth), and shan (compassion). In April 1999, in response to what was perceived as unfair government interference with the group, a large demonstration of at least 10,000 followers was organized in Beijing's Tiananmen Square, the site of a student demonstration and a bloody military crackdown just ten years earlier. Unnerved by this show of strength and the choice of location, the Chinese government quickly banned the movement, reacting with overwhelming force to arrest leaders and practitioners, and to this day opposes Falun Gong within China with crushing power that has received repeated accusations of human rights abuses. Despite this official reaction in its homeland, Falun Gong has multiple centers of practice around the world, particularly Western Europe and North America.

In terms of practices, Falun Gong is an excellent example of what Religious Studies scholars call a "syncretistic tradition," namely one that has formed from the borrowing of elements of preexisting religions, even as it adds newer, novel aspects. In his writings and then the beliefs of his followers, Li Hongzhi has brought together components of Buddhism, Daoism, Chinese folk traditions (especially qigong), strains of Christian biblical literalism, nineteenth-century esoteric movements like Theosophy, and even quantum physics. Most basically, Falun Gong begins from a premise similar to Chinese qigong, which is that the body is composed of energy channels that should be maintained and exercised through practiced breathing and bodily postures. Li Hongzhi's writings espouse five practices of stretches and movements meant to improve the body's health and the individual's spiritual awareness. These practices intersect with Buddhist meditation, as they incorporate meditative visualization and states, as well as Daoist concepts of balance through the harmony of *Yin* and *Yang*. Over time, these exercises are thought to rid the mind and body of impurities that block health and insight.

Falun Gong also holds to a multiversal, deity-filled cosmos and microverse that, once one is purified and adept enough, a practitioner is said to be able to experience. Awakened beings and bodhisattvas from Buddhist traditions and Immortals from Daoism, along with other entities from long-lost civilizations (such as Atlantis and the remote Himalayas) and even extraterrestrial creatures, are said to exist both out in the higher reaches of the cosmos as well as the microscopic world all around. These other dimensions, inspired by the notion in quantum physics of the multiverse, are thought to coincide with our reality. By using the prescribed physical exercises, meditating for focus, and renouncing worldly things, a person's inner eye and wheel of morality are said to open and all these surrounding worlds become visible to them. A rarified state of awareness (similar to the concept of awakening in Buddhism) is then thought to be possible for the adherent, and Li Hongzhi himself has been claimed to possess various supernormal powers.

Drawing explicitly (through references to some passages in the book of *Genesis* in the Hebrew Bible) on the notion of "original sin" propagated by some Christian denominations, Li Hongzhi and Falun Gong ascribe sickness, crime, and other misfortunes in the world to a fall from grace in a far earlier period of humanity. Controversially, though not unlike fundamentalist or militant strains of other religious traditions around the world, Li Hongzhi's writings and the movement in general take extremely conservative positions critical of the LGBTQ community, feminism, racial integration and interracial marriage, the scientific theory of evolution, and Western medicine, seeing these as forces that lead to the corruption of the modern world. From this extremely conservative point of view, Li Hongzhi and his followers believe the movement is a method for renewing the self and the world.

Scriptures and Festivals

The primary scriptures of the group are the writings of Li Hongzhi himself. In those works, though, Li quotes regularly from Buddhist, Daoist, and some Christian texts, connecting ideas from those religions with his own. (If the reader compares some of the ideas expressed in this chapter to the other chapters in this volume regarding Buddhism and Daoism, they will see the overlaps.) Some of Li's most frequently cited writings include Falun Gong, an introductory text that cites the comparisons between the group's practices and Buddhism and Daoism, and Zhuan Falun, which covers more of the meditative and physical practices.

Other than the acknowledged leadership of Li Hongzhi, Falun Gong expresses little hierarchical structure, eschewing many ritual practices one might find in other religious traditions, such as life cycle ceremonies or initiations. Instead, movement members engage in physical exercise and meditative practices alone or in groups, sometimes utilizing public places, including parks, as gathering areas. Members may also meet online, if a local community of fellow practitioners is lacking or unavailable. Group study sessions to read over and confer on Li Hongzhi's writings may occur on a regular basis and come the closest to qualifying as regular rituals or festivals in this tradition. Although the group is not known to widely proselytize, an additional regular activity is for small groups to share pamphlets on the movement or distribute these materials in public areas such as train stations and highway rest stops. Other ways that Falun Gong spreads its message, either directly or indirectly, are through the medium *The Epoch Times*, a highly conservative news outlet critical of the Chinese Communist Party, and the Shen Yun tours, that, billed as celebrations of ancient Chinese culture, similarly advance conservative values along with featuring dance and singing performances in tours across the United States.

Common Misunderstandings, Stereotypes, and Classroom Concerns

One of the most persistent stereotypes regarding Falun Gong is the term "cult," which possesses many negative connotations. Religious traditions of more recent origin (often termed "New Religious Movements" by scholars of Religious Studies), especially those with beliefs that can appear out of the mainstream, are sometimes labeled with this pejorative term which most Religious Studies experts tend to avoid. Importantly, as referenced frequently above, many elements of Falun Gong do parallel those found in older and more populous traditions. It may be helpful for instructors to compare Falun Gong, or other new religious movements they encounter, with other established religious traditions to find the commonalities before employing what can be derogatory terminology, such as the word "cult."

The political situation in China could prompt instructor concern, as the government's suppression of the movement has coincided with its widespread usage of the term "cult" to describe Falun Gong. Should a student of that perspective be in a classroom with a student who adheres to the beliefs of Falun Gong, tensions may arise. The instructor should be prepared in that situation to moderate any disputes. Additionally, given the extremely conservative views espoused by Falun Gong, as described above, the instructor should be prepared to moderate any tensions that occur on that basis, as those views can be problematic in a diverse, multicultural setting. Given the Falun Gong's resistance to Western medicine, in order to be as prepared as possible, the instructor should confer in advance with the student and necessary authorities about potential medical situations that might occur, discussing alternatives for various eventualities.

Culturally Responsive Pedagogy

With these beliefs and potential classroom issues in mind, there are ways to make students of the Falun Gong movement feel welcome in the classroom. One potential opportunity, depending on the subject matter being taught and the willingness of the student, is to discuss the importance of physical exercise and concentration and how these elements can promote physical as well as mental health, as these aspects are seen as conjoined in Falun Gong. If the instructor and student are willing, an assignment could even be crafted (within the confines of what is acceptable for the course) where the student could explore those connections.

Further Reading and Resources

Chang, Maria. *Falun Gong: The End of Days*. New Haven, CT: Yale University Press, 2004.

Lewis, James R. *Falun Gong*. Cambridge: Cambridge University Press, 2018.

Ming, Xiao. *The Cultural Economy of Falun Gong in China: A Rhetorical Perspective*. Columbia: University of South Carolina Press, 2011.

Ownby, David. *Falun Gong and the Future of China*. New York: Oxford University Press, 2008.

Palmer, David. *Qigong Fever: Body, Science, and Utopia in China*. New York: Cambridge University Press, 2007.

Porter, Noah. *Falun Gong in the United States: An Ethnographic Study*. Dissertation.com, 2003.

Tong, James. *Revenge of the Forbidden City: The Suppression of the Falun Gong in China, 1999–2005*. New York: Oxford University Press, 2009.

7

Chinese Religions: Traditional Chinese Religions

> One had seen the Yin Yang symbol on bumper stickers and tattoos. Another had seen it on the cover of a book entitled *The Dao of Parenting*. A third recalled hearing about Confucius from an episode of *Dinosaur Train* when he was younger. After a pause, another mentioned concepts found within the film *Crouching Tiger, Hidden Dragon*. As the students and I in my "Eastern Philosophy" class continued to discuss prior knowledge of the religions of China, it became apparent that even though there was little actual experience with these traditions, many students had had some exposure, even if only superficially, to key ideas related to these ways of thought, showing how global they have become in their reach.

Introduction

One of the first steps to understanding the religions of China is recognizing that boundaries between and within traditions can be virtually non-existent. While it is certainly possible to identify differences between the worldviews of the major Chinese traditions – namely Confucianism, Daoism, and various schools of Buddhism, leaving aside for now other movements such as

Falun Gong – practitioners themselves often blend elements of these religions together, borrowing and employing respective rituals and interposing beliefs as fit their circumstances. When this fact is placed alongside the longstanding existence of more diffuse practices (sometimes characterized as "popular religion"), the category of "Chinese religions" becomes more complicated than might originally be expected. With that in mind, loose estimates show that between 300 and 400 million people in the world may practice some or all aspects of these Chinese traditional religions.

In this chapter, we will provide a brief historical overview of ideas resting in common for all Chinese traditions, then focus individually on the practices and beliefs primarily of Confucianism and Daoism. Though Buddhism is an important religion in China, it has been covered in a separate chapter and we will only discuss it briefly, mainly to survey some of its particularly Chinese forms.

Before proceeding further, we need to make a note of language. There have been two primary ways of transliterating Chinese characters into Romanized scripts: the Wade-Giles system and Pinyin. The latter is more widely favored and this is the system we will use in this chapter. In places, though, one may see the Wade-Giles format still used, which accounts for variations in rendering some Chinese terms. For example: "Tao" (Wade-Giles) versus "Dao" (Pinyin).

Historical Overview

The civilizations of China are among the oldest in the world, extending back to the early settlements along the Yellow River, which archaeological evidence suggests could reach back as far as 12,000 BCE. Around 1,400 BCE, the time of the very early Shang Dynasty (the first Chinese dynasty), elements key to most later Chinese religious beliefs were already taking form. For instance, already by this time one's family lineage was assigned great importance. Deceased members of the family especially, the *ancestors*, were thought to exert a lasting influence on the lives of their descendants. Ritual practices such as divination and sacrifice were used to determine their desires and maintain their favor in this life. The same techniques were used to interact with other entities from the Tian, the heavenly realm, who could also impact events in the human world for good or ill.

Within and around these relationships was the concept of Yin and Yang, which expresses the variety of forms cosmic and earthly forces take amid an overall balance of energies. Yin is thought to exemplify darker, more passive energies found in elements such as earth, water, night, and the moon. Yang, on the other hand, represents the active, bright forces of sun, fire, and daylight. The Taijitu, the famous circular diagram, represents the interplay of these light and dark forces (Figure 7.1). These energies are present throughout nature, being found in greater and lesser ratios in various animals and humans. Creating and maintaining a balance between Yin and Yang principles contributes to personal and societal harmony, while energies out of joint can lead to chaos and calamity in those same realms.

FIGURE 7.1 The Taijitu, the famous circular diagram that symbolizes Yin and Yang forces

After the Shang Dynasty fell, the rulers of the Zhou Dynasty (eleventh to third century BCE) rose to power. During the course of the Zhou Dynasty, the relationships between the aforementioned concepts were strengthened. The Zhou rulers asserted that they had ascended to power due to the favor of the heavenly realm, a dispensation known as the "mandate of heaven" (Tianming) that would last as long as certain cosmic and worldly forces, including family and society, were kept in balance. Individuals and families could assist in upholding and strengthening this harmony by maintaining order in the family (Xiao, or filial piety) and devotion to their ancestors, which was extended to the ruling members of the dynasty. It is in this historical setting, with this philosophical and social background, that the religions of China we know today came into being.

Confucianism

The first of these traditions, Confucianism, is named after a thinker whose given name was actually Kong Qiu, but through a Western corruption of his name into Latin, has become known as "Confucius." He lived in northeastern China during the sixth to fifth centuries BCE, which was an era of the Zhou Dynasty known for a breakdown in social and political unity amid widespread unrest. Idealizing the early period of the Zhou as a kind of utopia of cohesion and order between the socio-political and family units, Confucius's writings were aimed primarily at recapturing and reestablishing that assumed former glory.

Though in his life Confucius most likely never rose above the station of a mid- to lower-level state bureaucrat, his ideas (largely collected in a text called the *Analects*) have had a longstanding impact not only in China, but also countries influenced by China, such as Vietnam, Korea, and Japan. For example, his scheme of social interaction, which is defined by a patriarchal structure called the Five Relationships, imagines bonds of obedience and obligation between pairs of established roles. These five key relationships, according to Confucius were:

Ruler to Subject
Father to Son
Husband to Wife
Elder to Younger Brother
Elder to Younger Friend

The individuals in the roles on the left-hand side were seen as the dominant parties in the relationship and the subservient ones on the right-hand side owed them obedience and deference. The dominant individuals only lived up to their roles, however, if they treated their subordinates with Ren, translated and understood as "benevolence," "empathy," or even sometimes rendered as "human-heartedness." For example, a ruler who failed to treat his subjects with appropriate benevolence might lose the right to be seen as a ruler, and hence forfeit the Tianming, or mandate of heaven. If rulers, fathers, husbands, and others embodied Ren, however, those in the subservient position owed them obedience, correlated to the Xiao of filial piety. If all parties observed their roles adequately, they would be acting in accord with Li, "ritual propriety" or correctness, which would emanate harmony and peace throughout society.

As a consequence, personally developing tendencies toward Ren and Li was incredibly important to Confucius's scheme. Continuous self-discipline and observance of the proper ritual behavior, Confucius argued, would lead eventually to sincere and almost spontaneous expressions of benevolence and filial piety. Literature, the arts, and music also contributed to higher moral character due to their capacity to refine one's thought. Eventually, over time, one who has perfected these qualities can be regarded as a Junzi, or "person of virtue" (sometimes rendered through the lens of patriarchy as the "gentleman"). Overall, in the Confucian perspective we see an emphasis on order, structure, and discipline, with an overarching theme of adherence to social principles.

Daoism

As its name suggests, the parallel tradition of Daoism is founded on the concept of the Dao, meaning "way" or "path." The Dao is seen as a primordial force pervading the universe itself. Beyond all distinctions and attributes, the Dao is experienced in the world as the differing qualities of Yin and Yang and these energies, when allowed to flow through a person in natural balance, bring one into closer alignment with the Dao. From the beginning there were various forms of Daoism which can be broadly broken into a more philosophically oriented school and a set of ritual-based practices meant to physically experience and manage the manifold energies of the Dao.

The philosophical school of Daoism is usually associated with the personality of Laozi, a figure about whom very little is actually known historically. A possible contemporary of Confucius during the sixth and fifth centuries BCE, Laozi is considered the author of one of the key texts of Daoism, the *Daodejing* ("The Book of the Way and Its Power"), though most scholars consider the book to have been composed by many individuals over time. Laozi, whether he existed historically or not, is still an important figure for Daoism as his solitude, purported wisdom, and connection to nature in many ways exemplify the ideal life from this tradition's point of view.

The *Daodejing* puts forward these very points by repeatedly emphasizing that the Dao, being the summation and encapsulation of all that exists, cannot be described or expressed through language. Attempts to do so, according to this text, actually take one further away from the true Dao. Instead, the Dao can only be experienced in quietude and often isolation, when a person follows his or her in-born talents and inclinations, especially in communing with the natural world. From this vantage, and in contrast to Confucianism, virtue is entirely spontaneous and does not need to be cultivated. States of harmony – whether collective or individual – can best be achieved by Wuwei, literally "non-action," when individual behavior is free and not coerced, as opposed to disciplined and formalized.

Ritualized Daoism focuses more on lived experience and consists largely of practices that may have been culled from popular customs and traditions extending back as far as the ancient Shang Dynasty. Many of these rituals are based on managing, increasing, or balancing the flow of Yin and Yang in the body or the immediate environment. Taiji and Qigong, which are composed of martial arts-based bodily movements and breath exercises, are ways of monitoring the flow of one's bodily energies, just as Feng Shui does the same for the composition and arrangement of Yin and Yang energies in a room or dwelling. There are established traditions with ritualized Daoism of figures who have mastered the control of these energies to the point where they have achieved incredible longevity and are thus termed Immortals. Chinese establishments and homes will often have shrines, images, or other ornaments related to these figures who are exemplars of Daoist practice. Within ritualized Daoism there is also an established priesthood who oversees these practices and will also intercede for individuals and families experiencing illness or other difficulties potentially connected to imbalances of Yin and Yang. As with Confucianism, Daoist ideas have spread into other areas of Asia, including Vietnam, Korea, and Japan, as well as Taiwan.

Chinese Buddhism

As mentioned previously, Buddhism has been covered in another chapter, but there are a few schools of Buddhist thought that originate in China that are worth a brief mention. For instance, Ch'an (the "meditation" school) originated in China around the sixth century CE and went on to assume the form of Zen in Japan. Though originally founded in India, Pure Land Buddhism became immensely popular in China following the second century CE. In this form of Buddhism, various Buddhas and Buddhas-to-be use their powers to create other-dimensional worlds for the benefit of Buddhists, who can reach these realms through recitations and other devotions. In an example of the cross-pollination between traditions, these Buddhas and Buddhas-to-be (such as Kuan-Yin and Amitabha) were frequently associated or even identified with Daoist Immortals. The Buddha Maitreya is perhaps the most famous example, as in China his imagery is melded with Daoist and other traditions to create the so-called "fat happy laughing Buddha," also called Budai.

Scriptures and Festivals

Key scriptures for Chinese religions include the following, broken down by tradition.

Confucianism
The "Five Classics"

The Book of Changes (I Ching)
The Book of Poetry
The Book of Documents
The Book of Rites
Spring and Autumnal Annals

The "Four Books"

Analects
Mencius
Great Learning
Doctrine of the Mean

Daoism
Daodejing
Zhuangzi

Buddhism
Platform Sutra of the Sixth Patriarch (Ch'an text)
The Three Pure Land Scriptures

There are also many popular festivals celebrated across Chinese traditions. Veneration of ancestors is a common recurring theme and festivals take place at the same annual intervals in a calendar based on the lunar system. For example, festivals in the seventh and tenth months focus on offerings to ancestors, both in public and also in private family abodes. Festivals during the third and fourth months celebrate the birthdays of certain Immortals as well as the Buddha. The most famous and popular festival by far, though, is the New Year celebration, which combines rites important to family and society.

Common Misunderstandings, Stereotypes, and Classroom Concerns

A first point to be wary of in this category is the aforementioned interconnection between the Chinese traditions discussed. Unlike other traditions (such as Christianity, Judaism, or Islam) where religious identities are considered exclusive, it has long been the case in Chinese culture that individuals and communities will blend Confucian, Daoist, and Buddhist ideas and practices. In fact, one popular image in Chinese art depicts Confucius, Laozi, and the Buddha together as the "Three Sages," each a teacher on an equal level with the others. In this way, all three traditions are seen as making valuable contributions to human understanding. Those of Chinese background will not likely identify exclusively with one or the other tradition.

Second, one should be wary of common stereotypes of Chinese culture that have emerged largely due to misconstrued aspects of each of these religions. The Confucian *Analects*, for example, is constructed largely as a series of short aphorisms which has been unfortunately dismissed at times as or likened to "fortune cookie" sayings. These kinds of jokes should obviously be avoided. Similarly, Daoist-inflected practices such as Taiji may lend the impression that all those of a Chinese background are adepts in the martial arts. In reality, Confucianism and Daoism represent a sophisticated combination of philosophy, ritual, politics, and ethics beyond what these superficial interpretations suggest.

Third, perhaps owing to the Confucian ideal of studious self-improvement through education and the desire to please one's family and ancestors, the stereotype has developed that students of Chinese ancestry are expected to be extremely intelligent and hardworking. Needless to say, these kinds of generalizations regarding individuals based on cultural background should be avoided.

Finally, religion itself has at times been a fraught topic in China, especially during the period of decades following the founding of the Communist People's Republic of China under Mao Zedong in 1949. That regime over time attempted to deemphasize religious figures and practices, particularly during the period of the Cultural Revolution (1966–1976). Though there are signs of a contemporary revival of Confucian, Daoist, and some Buddhist practices in twenty-first-century China, this has primarily been the case when the tradition or ritual involved has been deemed non-threatening to the power or authority of the state. In other cases, such as Tibetan Buddhism (which is seen as undermining Chinese control of Tibet) or Falun Gong (a movement founded substantially on Qigong practices which has at times flouted governmental orders), religious traditions have still been regarded as potential threats to societal order and in need of strict regulation. This dynamic tension between religion and politics in China should be kept in mind.

Culturally Responsive Pedagogy

A teacher with students in the classroom from a Chinese background can take several steps to ensure a culturally responsive environment. First, instructors can make certain that the cultural background of Chinese students is present in the classroom. For example, in social studies or history classes, one could be sure to include key figures in Chinese history discussed above, such as Confucius, as well as to make sure to reference ancient Chinese civilization alongside the ancient Mesopotamians, for instance. In art classes, one could draw on Chinese calligraphy or Daoist nature scenes to represent Chinese cultural achievements. In literature, excerpts from the *Daodejing* or *Journey to the West* by Wu

Cheng'en, a classic sixteenth-century Chinese novel that blends Buddhist thought with Confucian and Daoist principles, would help in representing Chinese cultural contributions in literature.

A second strategy for culturally responsive pedagogy with Chinese students is to draw from their prior knowledge and experience, while being careful to make certain that individuals do not feel pressured to share. Relative to the traditions discussed in this chapter, students might be inclined to share stories regarding their own family dynamics and upbringing or experiences with traditional medicinal or meditative practices. Assignments or presentations could also be crafted in such a way that Chinese students could connect them to their traditions and share their experiences in the ways most comfortable to them. Inclusion of Chinese ideas, texts, history, and the experiences of individual students in these kinds of ways could serve to help better incorporate Chinese students or students from a Chinese background into the classroom.

Further Reading and Resources

Adler, Joseph. *Chinese Religious Traditions*. New York: Prentice Hall, 2002.

Bokenkamp, Stephen R. *Early Daoist Scriptures*. Berkeley: University of California Press, 1997.

Ch'en, Kenneth. *The Chinese Transformation of Buddhism*. Princeton, NJ: Princeton University Press, 1973.

Ch'en, Kenneth. *Buddhism in China: A Historical Survey*. Princeton, NJ: Princeton University Press, 1964.

Confucius: The Analects. Translated by D.C. Lau. Harmondsworth: Penguin Books, 1979.

I Ching: The Book of Change. Translated by Thomas Cleary. Berkeley, CA: Shambhala, 1992.

Kohn, Livia. *Introducing Daoism*. London and New York: Routledge, 2008.

Lao Tzu: Tao Te Ching. Translated by D. C. Lau. Harmondsworth: Penguin Books, 1964.

Poceski, Mario. *Introducing Chinese Religions*. London and New York: Routledge, 2009.

Watson, Burton. *Zhuangzi: Basic Writings*. Translated by Burton Watson. New York: Columbia University Press, 1996.

8

Christianity: Overview

Christianity had its origins two millennia ago in the Middle East, when a prophet arose within Palestine – previously known as Israel – in the eastern part of the Roman Empire. Jesus of Nazareth embarked on a mission of preaching and healing which convinced many of his fellow Jews that he was the Messiah, a long-expected deliverer who would free the Hebrew people from bondage. After his arrest, crucifixion, and death at the hands of Roman authorities, his followers believed that he had been resurrected from the dead and had commissioned them to spread his message of deliverance and redemption. His life and work were recorded in what became known as the New Testament. Combined with the Hebrew Scripture – known among Christians, but not Jews, as the Old Testament – to form what came to be known as the Bible (Greek, "the books").

Although this new religion soon underwent divisions that have lasted to the present day, certain features rapidly emerged that provided a center for this emergent religious tradition.

1. Central to this unity has always been the historical and spiritual figure of Jesus, known as the Christ (the "anointed one"), who is the final revealer of the will of God the Father and the mediator between the Father and humanity. The exact nature of Jesus – divine and/

DOI: 10.4324/9781003405894-8

or human – has provoked considerable debate among Christians over the centuries.
2. Shared by most Christians is a belief in the Trinity: one God in three "persons," namely, the Father (creator), Son (redeemer), and Holy Spirit (sanctifier).
3. These and other basic theological propositions were codified in the creeds – statements of belief by the early Christian community. These creeds, of which the Apostles and the Nicene are still widely used today, were enunciated definitively in the declarations of the early ecumenical – worldwide – councils of bishops that took place periodically throughout the entire Christian world between 325 and 451 CE.

During the following two millennia, the religion known as Christianity spread rapidly, first within the vast Roman Empire, then throughout Europe and, eventually, the entire world, following the paths of European imperial expansion. Major events in its history were:

- the ending of persecution and granting of official recognition by Emperor Constantine in the early fourth century.
- the division of the Roman Empire at the same time into eastern and western zones. In each of these would arise separate versions of the religion, with Rome and Constantinople/Byzantium as major centers. (These two centers formally separated in 1054, with the Pope at Rome and the Patriarch of Constantinople mutually excommunicating one another.)
- expansion into the "New World" and beyond in the wake of English, French, Portuguese, and Spanish imperial expansion in the fifteenth and sixteenth centuries.
- the splitting of Christianity in Western and Central Europe during the Reformation(s) of the early sixteenth century into "Protestant" movements rejecting the authority of the Pope and Roman Catholics continuing to recognize that authority.

By the time that Europeans were beginning to colonize the eastern coast of North America, Christianity had become fragmented into Roman Catholicism – here, mainly English, French, and Spanish – and Protestantism, a sort of umbrella term that included those movements led by Martin Luther in Germany, John Calvin and others in Switzerland, the Tudor Dynasty in Britain, and a variety of radical local leaders in the Rhine Valley. These movements morphed into what are still known as the Lutheran, Reformed, Anglican, and Anabaptist strains of Protestant Christianity. United mainly by a rejection of the authority of the Pope in favor of that of the Bible, they took on new identities and directions in the New World context.

European Christians settling in North America usually did so in the context of geography and politics. Puritans – Reformed/Calvinist Protestants rejecting the authority of the British monarchy over religious life – dominated in New England, while their Presbyterian (Scottish Calvinist) cousins centered in the Middle Colonies. Roman Catholics were originally entrenched in Maryland; after being overthrown by Anglicans, they nevertheless flourished in the Baltimore and Philadelphia areas. The Church of England (Anglicans), supported by the British government, dominated the New York City region and much of the South, especially Virginia. Quakers, a radical British movement, were endowed with the Pennsylvania colony, to which their leader William Penn recruited similarly pacifist Anabaptist groups – Amish, Brethren, Mennonites – to become compatible neighbors. Lutherans from Germany would also settle among their ethnic counterparts in the "Keystone State."

The religious and ethnic pluralism that was already established by the time of American independence from Britain posed new dilemmas in the New Republic. Puritan Congregationalists in New England and Anglicans in New York and the South had become accustomed to an "establishment" status, by which they were recognized as "official" by colonial governments and thus entitled to financial support and social privilege. Rhode Island, which Baptist Roger Williams had earlier founded as a place of religious liberty for dissenters such as himself, and Pennsylvania were the only two colonies where such liberty was acknowledged by law. The situation of minority groups such as Catholics and Jews was usually dependent on local circumstances.

The Founding Fathers, when framing the Constitution and the subsequent Bill of Rights, had to confront an unprecedented situation in which religious affiliation was de facto – in fact – pluralistic, but in which the standing of these groups had been subject to a patchwork of legal and political situations. What to do? The framers of America's fundamental laws were subject to pressures from three different directions. First, *de facto* pluralism was very real. Should the Founders have chosen to "establish" a national religion, which would they choose, since no single group enjoyed majority status? Second, dissenting groups such as Baptists, which had never enjoyed established status, lobbied vigorously for an acknowledgment of *de jure* – legal – pluralism, since they had been forced previously to provide financial support through taxation to churches from which they felt alienated. Third, Enlightenment-influenced skeptics about traditional Christianity, such as Ben Franklin, Thomas Jefferson, and Tom Paine, opposed governmental recognition and support for any particular religion, fearing that such recognition would corrupt both the government and the religions thus favored. (The close relationship between the Catholic Church and the Bourbon monarchy in France, culminating in the bloody French Revolution, was a dramatic and cautionary example of where such collaboration might lead.)

The resolution of this vexing question came in the form of a truly revolutionary innovation: the First Amendment to the Constitution in 1791. In addition to guaranteeing fundamental rights such as speech and assembly, this first article of the "Bill of Rights" resolved the issue of the relationship of "Church" and "State" as follows:

> *Congress shall make no law respecting an establishment of religion, or prohibiting the free exercise thereof.*

Freedom of religion was thus established as one of the core principles of the new republic. The devil, as it turned out, would be in the details, as interpreted over the ensuing centuries through a plethora of Supreme Court decisions as to how this broad principle was to be applied in an ever-unfolding succession of particular cases, often occasioned by self-marginalized sectarian groups. These included Quakers and other "peace" churches arguing for conscientious objection to military service, Jehovah's Witnesses claiming exemption from saluting the flag in public schools, and Amish rejecting formal education for their children beyond the sixth grade. The question, especially in public schools, as to whether particular religious practices should be exempted from rules intended to impose uniform behaviors is perennial and most likely never fully resolvable. (COVID vaccination and mask-wearing is an apt contemporary example.)

The decades between Independence and World War I witnessed tumultuous and unceasing changes to the national religious landscape. Native American peoples were relentlessly pushed westward, carrying and adapting their religious traditions as they were thus removed. Enslaved Africans were converted under duress to Christianity in large numbers, but combined it with African remembrances while adapting to new circumstances. The opening up of the West for Euro-American colonization coincided with a major new movement, the Latter-day Saints (Mormons), establishing a new society in the Utah desert where the practice of polygamy would raise countless problems until resolved with Utah's admission as a state in 1896.

European immigration had the largest impact on religious diversity, though. Waves of newcomers from the British Isles and Dutch and French Protestants were supplemented – in some places overwhelmed – by German and Scandinavian Lutherans; Irish, Polish, Slovak, and Italian Catholics; and Orthodox Christians from Eastern Europe, Greece, and the Balkans. Jews, who had reposed in tiny enclaves along the East Coast in colonial times, now grew rapidly first among German-speakers and, after the Civil War, by new Yiddish-speaking waves from the Russian Empire. By the time of World War I, America's cities had become melting pots of "others," feared and loathed by many old-stock Protestants even while providing cheap labor for a bustling economy.

The 1920s saw a national in-turning as Congress passed a series of acts sharply limiting immigration from Europe beyond northwestern Protestant-dominant areas. (Asian immigration had been virtually extinguished prior to World War I.) Anti-immigrant groups promoted ideologies, sometimes based on specious eugenics theory that promoted restrictive laws and sometimes violence against Catholics and Jews as well as Blacks. World War II brought about greater inter-ethnic mixing in the military, and the 1942 GI Bill of Rights opened up broad new educational and career opportunities for returning (White) veterans.

As "Protestant-Catholic-Jew" became the expanded formulation for the American religious spectrum in the 1950s, the following decade saw an even greater challenge to national tolerance for pluralism. The Hart-Celler Immigration Reform Act of 1965 opened the way for Buddhists, Hindus, Muslims, Sikhs, and other religionists concentrated in Asia and the Middle East. The Civil Rights Acts of the same era brought African American Christianity into the public spotlight, as well as new Black religious movements such as the Nation of Islam. Growing immigration from Mexico, Cuba, Puerto Rico, and other Spanish-speaking lands brought with it a new influx of Catholics with their own folk and national variations on that tradition, as well as considerable numbers of Pentecostals and other Evangelicals.

Reactions to these newcomers emerged among a newly forming Religious Right, resurrecting the nativist themes of the 1920s and the nineteenth century, but now including assimilated Catholics as well as Fundamentalist Protestants. A vast array of religious traditions coexist and contend in the contemporary public sphere. Unfortunately, teachers and school administrators are often caught in the middle of disputes over religious identity.

Further Reading and Resources

Ahlstrom, Sydney E. *A Religious History of the American People.* New Haven, CT: Yale University Press, 1973.

Cross, F. L., ed. *The Oxford Dictionary of the Christian Church.* Oxford: Oxford University Press, 1983.

Diarmaid MacCulloch. *A History of Christianity: The First Three Thousand Years*. New York: Viking, 2009.

McManners, John, ed. *The Oxford Illustrated History of Christianity*. Oxford and New York: Oxford University Press, 1990.

Williams, Peter W. *America's Religions* (4th ed.). Urbana, IL: University of Illinois Press, 2015.

9

Christianity: Amish, Mennonite, and Other Anabaptist-Descended Churches

A 17-year-old living in an Old Order Amish community in Lancaster County, Pennsylvania opts for baptism after going through a discernment process to decide if she will be baptized and remain Amish or join "the English" world. In a large home that has been cleaned and prepared for the occasion, she goes through baptism with a group of other young people, some of whom have been waiting for a year for a critical mass of young people ready for baptism to form. Their baptism will be done as a group. Baptism by consenting adults is the ritual that marks lifetime membership in an Anabaptist community. For young people in Old Order Amish communities, this entails leaving formal schooling and completing vocational education. Girls and young women learn domestic arts along with some agricultural skills while boys specialize in farming.

Introduction

The estimated population of the Amish of North America (adults and children) as of June 2024 was 400,910.[1] Mennonites in the United States numbered 500,481 as of 2018.[2]

Historical Overview

Together, the Lutheran, Reformed (Calvinist), and Anglican traditions are sometimes spoken of as the *Magisterial Reformation*, or reform "from the top down" through the will of the ruling classes. A fourth and much more diffuse part is the *Radical Reformation*, a very loose collection of local movements that arose in the Rhine Valley (Germany and Switzerland) beginning in the 1520s. Although these movements varied considerably in beliefs and practices, they shared a common rejection of any role that might be played by the civil government in Christian life. Usually pacifist on biblical grounds, they were fiercely persecuted by the governments whose authority they had rejected, and most disappeared quickly.

Among the survivors of these persecutions were two closely related groups that arose in Switzerland in the 1530s, the Amish and the Mennonites. The Amish, named after their leader Jakob Amman, believed they were following a version of Christianity based directly on the original teachings of Jesus, which included a rejection of violence and, more broadly, "worldliness." The Mennonites were a break-off group, led by Menno Simons, which rejected what they regarded as excessively harsh Amish practices such as "banning" and "shunning" dissenters. These and similar groups were recruited by Quaker leader William Penn to join his new colony, Pennsylvania, in the early 1700s, since they shared ideals of peaceable living. About two dozen sects of Amish and Mennonites developed as they pursued their traditional agricultural lifestyles in Ohio, Indiana, and Wisconsin as well as Pennsylvania. Although the Mennonites and, to a lesser extent, the Amish, have become more open to accommodations with modern society, their most conservative branches still reject modern technology (except for business purposes) as well as education beyond the primary and middle school level. Their pacifism and other distinctive beliefs have fueled many court cases involving Church/State separation, and have usually been successful.

"Peace churches," preeminently Amish and Mennonites, share the Quaker commitment to peace, but vary considerably in their local cultures. Amish, found in Pennsylvania and Ohio especially, have historically distanced themselves from "English" society, and maintain a culture rooted in farming and handcrafts. In the landmark 1972 Supreme Court case of Wisconsin vs. Yoder, the court's majority decision supported the rights of Old Order Amish parents to remove children from public schools before the age of 18. One justice wrote a dissenting opinion that focused on children's rights to determine their future, but nevertheless voted with the majority. The U.S. law has generally supported the practice of Anabaptist parents to end their children's schooling with the eighth grade. Mennonites, while pacifist, have integrated more fully into the dominant society. Mennonite children tend to be more integrated into public school settings and continue public schooling well beyond middle school.

Scriptures, Holidays, and Worship

Amish and Mennonites regard the Hebrew and Christian scriptures as authoritative, but also value accounts of the martyrdoms of their Reformation-era ancestors. Worship is conducted in family homes, with no separate buildings for the purpose. Major Christian holidays such as Christmas and Easter are observed festively. Mennonite worship takes place in church buildings and follows more traditional Protestant practices.

Common Misunderstandings, Stereotypes, and Classroom Concerns

Although the Amish try to insulate themselves from "worldly" influences such as modern technology, they practice this more strictly in their homes than in commercial relations with the larger English world. They also reject secondary education for their children as "worldly." Mennonites, though they share pacificism and a preference for a simple life with their Amish cousins, live in the broader world without distinctive clothing.

Culturally Responsive Pedagogy

In areas such as sections of Indiana, Ohio, and Pennsylvania, where Amish and Mennonites congregate, field trips may be a possibility. Videos such as those produced by American Experience may provoke discussions as to how and why some religious groups chose to distance themselves from full participation in "worldly" American life and how they are able to maintain this distance.

Notes

1. "Amish Population Profile, 2024," Young Center for Anabaptist and Pietist Studies, Elizabethtown College, https://groups.etown.edu/amishstudies/statistics/amish-population-profile-2024.
2. Mennonite World Conference, World Directory, 2018, p. 58.

Further Reading and Resources

"Amish America: Exploring Amish Culture and Communities," a resource by Erik Wesner. https://amishamerica.com/

"Amish America YouTube Channel," a resource created by Erik Wesner. https://www.youtube.com/c/AmishAmerica

"Amish." *American Experience*. https://www.youtube.com/watch?v=iSOn7NXWTbk

Amish Studies, an academic website developed by the Young Center for Anabaptist and Pietist Studies at Elizabethtown College to provide reliable information on Amish life and culture. Designed to assist scholars, students and the general public, the site was developed with support from the National Endowment for the Humanities.

https://groups.etown.edu/amishstudies/social-organization/education/

Dewalt, Mark W. *Amish Education in the United States and Canada.* Lanham, MD: Rowman and Littlefield Education, 2006.

Fisher, Sara E., and Rachel K. Stahl. *The Amish School.* Intercourse, PA: Good Books, 1997.

Hurst, Charles E., and David L. McConnell. *An Amish Paradox: Diversity and Change in the World's Largest Amish Community.* Baltimore, MD: Johns Hopkins University Press, 2010.

"Inside the Amish and Mennonite Communities: Living Plain," a documentary about the Amish and Mennonite population of Lancaster county in eastern Pennsylvania. https://www.youtube.com/watch?v=FwL_evg5z1I

Johnson-Weiner, Karen. *Train Up a Child: Old Order Amish and Mennonite Schools.* Baltimore, MD: Johns Hopkins University Press, 2007.

Lippy, Charles H., and Peter W. Williams, eds. *Encyclopedia of Religion in America.* Washington, DC: CQ Press, 2010, articles on "Anabaptist Denominational Family" (I, 75–82) and "Anabaptists" (I, 83–88).

"Mennonites." Wikipedia: The Free Encyclopedia. https://en.wikipedia.org/wiki/Mennonites

10

Christianity: Anglican and Episcopal

> Upon first visiting an Episcopal Church, someone not familiar with the denomination might find themselves puzzled. The church might be named after a saint (or not), and perhaps have a few statues or stained-glass windows depicting holy figures from the Christian tradition, such as the Apostles. At first they might think they were in a Roman Catholic Church, but would probably not see Stations of the Cross on the walls or shrines to the Virgin Mary, unless they had arrived at an Episcopal Church calling itself Anglo-Catholic. They would see a good-sized pulpit, altar, and baptismal font. They would most likely have found themselves in an Episcopal Church, neither fully Roman Catholic nor Protestant, but incorporating features from both traditions.

Membership

The membership of The Episcopal Church today is about 1.6 million, down, like most "mainline" churches, dramatically from the mid-twentieth century.[1] A smaller, more conservative split-off is the Anglican Church in North America (ca. 134,000 members), founded in 2009 in opposition to the ordination of gay clergy and other issues.[2]

Historical Overview

Anglicanism began as a variety of reformed/Protestant Christianity influenced by but differing in significance from the Lutheran and Calvinist/Reformed movements that arose early in the sixteenth century in England, which had recently undergone political consolidation by the Tudor monarchs, Henry VII and Henry VIII. The story of the latter monarch and his six wives is famous enough, and his marital difficulties helped launch religious reform in that nation. Henry first married Catherine of Aragon in 1509, but became disenchanted with the marriage and petitioned the Pope for an annulment – marital dissolution – so that he could pursue his second wife-to-be, Anne Boleyn. When the Pope refused, Henry defied him and declared himself to have sole authority over the Christian Church in England. Under Henry and two of his children, Edward VI and Elizabeth I, the Church of England gradually took shape as an independent national church, retaining priests, bishops, and an order of worship similar to that of the Catholic Church, but rejecting the authority of the Pope.

The Church of England was the first institutional embodiment of the strain of Christianity that later became known as *Anglicanism*, which presented itself as a "bridge church" by incorporating elements of governance, worship, and belief from both Roman Catholic and other Protestant traditions. (The term "Protestant" is no longer used by many Anglicans.) Distinctive components of Anglican religious culture are the *Authorized (King James) Version* of the English Bible of 1611 and the *Book of Common Prayer*, the English-language liturgy (order of public worship) compiled by Archbishop Thomas Cranmer and first issued in 1549. The influence of these two documents on the English language has spread far beyond the realm of religion over the centuries.

The Church of England and the Anglican form of Christianity soon became global as the British Empire expanded throughout the entire world in the ensuing centuries. In the North American colonies it was particularly strong in the New York City area as well as in most of the South, especially Virginia. Its status as an "established" – government supported – church made it a target during and after the Revolution, as many of its clergy fled after remaining loyal to the English government, and the notion of establishment was no longer in favor of the new nation. In 1784 the first bishop was chosen for the Protestant Episcopal Church, which was formally organized in 1789. (*Bishop* is a term used by many Christians as a title for regional religious leaders. *Episcopal* means having bishops as a central component of a governance system, or polity.)

What is now known officially as *The Episcopal Church* is the direct descendant of the Church of England, which had been legally established in many of the colonies – especially in the South – prior to Independence. The established character of the Church of England made it necessary that clergy and bishops take oaths of loyalty to the king or queen, who was (and still is) legally the head of the national church. Since this was not a possibility in the New Nation, those Anglican clergy who had not fled to Britain or Canada gathered in Philadelphia in 1789 – simultaneous with the framers of the Constitution – to found what was originally named The Protestant Episcopal Church. (The term "Protestant" was quietly dropped some time ago.) This new denomination featured a bicameral legislative body, similar to that of the United States, as well as an *episcopal* system of *polity* (governance), that is, with *bishops* presiding over regional *dioceses* made up of local *parishes*, in many ways resembling that of the Roman Catholic Church.

From its early days, the Episcopal Church has been regarded by many – with some justification – as the religious province of "the rich, the well-born, and the able." The early "Virginia Dynasty" of American presidents was entirely composed of at least nominal Episcopalians – Washington, Jefferson, Madison, Monroe – as was the case with Hamilton, John Jay, and a plurality of subsequent presidents (Franklin Roosevelt, George H. W. Bush), and Supreme Court justices. By the "Gilded Age" of the later nineteenth century, it had become the denomination of choice for many of the newly rich, such as the "Robber Barons" who had become the titans of industry. This was the era of a great campaign of church and cathedral building, boarding school foundings, and a well-funded more general program of cultural philanthropy.

Like other mainline denominations, membership in the Episcopal Church peaked in the 1960s and since then has experienced a precipitous decline correlating with controversies over race, gender, and sexual orientation similar to that experienced among the other "mainline" denominations. Although it remains prestigious regionally among old-line gentry, its emphasis on inclusiveness and social change has made it vulnerable to defections among conservatives. Its churches, many of them flourishing locally, stand as impressive monuments in many cities, but its appeal beyond the urban and suburban contexts is small today.

Scripture and Holidays

Episcopalians observe many of the same holidays as other "liturgical denominations" (Lutheran, Roman Catholic), but do not ask for any exemptions from school attendance. They follow the same set of scriptures as most, allowing for a range of translations. It follows the common lectionary – selections of scripture readings – over a three-cycle for use in worship. Christmas is a particularly important observance, since Episcopalians stress the doctrine of the Incarnation, that is, that Jesus took on human form and lived on earth.

Misunderstandings, Stereotypes, and Classroom Concerns

In earlier decades, Episcopalians were often seen as affluent and snobbish and fond of strong drinks, especially sherry and Scotch. They often were accused of being overly fond of English culture, and adopting "posh" accents. Contemporary Episcopalians tend to have higher educational and financial status than most other denominations, they now emphasize social outreach and downplay any elite status.

Culturally Responsive Pedagogy

Visiting an Episcopal Church and examining the architecture, the art, and the apparatus utilized for worship is a good introduction to its distinctive emphasis on the sacraments.

Notes

1. The Episcopal Church, https://www.episcopalchurch.org/about-us/.
2. Anglican Church in North America, https://www.always-forward.com/anglican-church-in-north-america.

Further Reading and Resources

Holmes, David L. *A Brief History of the Episcopal Church*. Harrisburg, PA: Trinity Press International, 1993.

Prichard, Robert W. *A History of the Episcopal Church* (3rd ed., rev.). Harrisburg, PA: Morehouse, 2014.

Williams, Peter W. *Religion, Art, and Money: Episcopalians and American Culture from the Civil War to the Great Depression*. Chapel Hill: University of North Carolina Press, 2015.

11

Christianity: Baptist

Introduction

Membership Statistics

American Baptist Churches 1,211,744 (2023)[1]
Southern Baptist Convention 12,982,090 (2024)[2]

> As the American frontier began to be settled during the early nineteenth century, it was said that "the Baptists came on foot, the Methodists came on horseback, and the Episcopalians came in parlor cars." At that time, American Protestant denominations were clearly differentiated not only by belief and worship but by social class as well. Today Baptists are one of America's largest religious traditions, and range in size from enormous wealthy megachurches to tiny rural "family churches."

Historical Overview

When many people today hear the word "Baptist," they assume it means "Southern Baptist" and therefore extremely conservative.

DOI: 10.4324/9781003405894-11

(The same applies to "Christian," which many – including reputable journalists – use misleadingly as a synonym for "Evangelical Christian.") Baptists actually come in a variety of flavors, due in part to their highly decentralized polity, in which each congregation is at least theoretically independent of all others.

In addition to the gigantic Southern Baptist Convention, however, there are Independent Baptists, who are generally similar to although even more independent than the SBC; African American Baptists (discussed below); any number of small churches with widely and wildly differing theologies and practices; and, within the Mainline spectrum, American – formerly Northern – Baptists.

Baptists in America usually trace their origins to Roger Williams, a dissident New England Puritan expelled from the Massachusetts Bay Colony in 1638 because of his opposition to infant baptism and the close relationship between church and state that typified the Puritan commonwealths. Opposition to the baptism of infants originated among the Anabaptists of the Reformation era (early 1500s), but the most immediate influence on New Englanders originated at the edges of the Puritan movement in Britain a century or more later. Baptists maintained that the Puritans were inconsistent in teaching that infants could be baptized even if they were not old enough to have experienced conversion.

The small congregation founded in Providence, Rhode Island, by Williams and other dissenters prospered over the decades, and by the time of Independence was able to erect the stately edifice that now stands next to the campus of Baptist-founded Brown University. As the nineteenth century wore on, Baptists spread widely in the South, and the loosely organized movement split in 1845 between slave-holding Southerners and abolitionist-leaning Northerners. Further splits occurred in the early twentieth century as many Northern Baptists allied themselves with the emergent Fundamentalist movement.

The Northern Baptists dropped "Northern" from their name in 1950, and today are known as the American Baptist Churches, USA. (Baptists reject the term "Church" as a denominational description, since their congregational polity is based on the belief that the term is applicable only to each local congregation.) They are a small denomination with close relations to other Mainline groups including the Disciples of Christ, the United Church of Christ, and the Presbyterian Church (USA). American Baptists differ from other mainline groups mainly in their adherence to adult baptism by immersion.

Southern Baptists today are the largest American denomination other than Roman Catholicism. Its members are overwhelmingly Evangelical or fundamentalist, although Christians embracing those descriptions can be found in a variety of denominations and independent churches. Conservative Protestants – Evangelicals of all sorts, including fundamentalists and Pentecostals – have for the past century been defining themselves in counterpoint to their Mainline (more liberal) counterparts. Evangelicalism first emerged as a distinctive religious movement during the 1740s, when George Whitefield and a host of imitators began to introduce a style of fervent preaching aimed not at teaching doctrine but rather inducing an emotional experience of conversion among their auditors. By the early nineteenth century, a series of "awakenings" had spread throughout various parts of the country, in which this *revivalist* style of preaching became standard.

During the nineteenth century Evangelicalism – never itself a denomination, although the term appears in some denominational names – dominated the Baptist, Methodist, and Presbyterian clusters, and its influence had an impact among some Congregationalists, Episcopalians, and Lutherans. Evangelical activists organized interdenominational societies, such as the "Benevolent Empire" of the 1820s, to distribute Bibles and tracts and also to bring about social change, especially the abolition of slavery. After the Civil War, the prohibition of the manufacture and sale of alcohol became the focus of organizing and lobbying efforts, culminating in 1919 in the 18th Amendment inaugurating national Prohibition. Evangelicals, however, did not concern themselves overly much with the social issues of the newly burgeoning cities, focusing instead on the suppression of vice – especially saloons – and the conversion of individuals.

Evangelicalism by the turn of the twentieth century had developed a core of beliefs and practices which still characterize it in the present day:

1. *Personal Conversion*. Participation in Evangelical worship is aimed at a *born-again* experience of God's grace working vividly in one's soul, and afterwards sustaining one's conversion in a life of grace.
2. *Biblical Authority*. The Hebrew and Christian Scriptures are wholly accurate, and contain the fullness of knowledge necessary for salvation. Other religions and scriptures are devoid of saving truth.
3. *Crucicentrism*. Jesus's death on the cross (from Latin *crux*) is the center and turning point of God's message of salvation for believers.
4. *The Missionary Imperative*. All believers are expected not simply to be content with their personal experience of salvation but also to actively try to convert others to the saving message of the Gospel.

Evangelicalism today is a major force on the American religious scene. The evangelist/revivalist Billy Graham came to national attention in the late 1940s with his message of the imminent return of Jesus, later modified to a focus on the personal experience of being "born again." Jimmy Carter's proclamation of his Evangelical identity during the 1976 presidential campaign further brought the movement into the national arena when prominent media proclaimed that time to be "the Year of the Evangelical." Evangelical scholars also began to reach beyond such institutions as Bible institutes into more mainstream colleges and seminaries, producing research comparable to that of prominent Mainline and secular universities, and critical of their own traditions.

Organizationally, Evangelicals tend toward a congregational polity, although those in the Wesleyan lineage may have a more hierarchical organization involving bishops. The largest denomination by far is the Southern Baptist Convention (SBC), which underwent an upheaval during the late 1970s in which Fundamentalists seized control of the denomination's seminaries and other agencies. This coup shifted power previously exercised by local churches into the hands of the Annual Convention, and resulted in the barring from membership of congregations that violated rules such as those forbidding the ordination of women. Although national leadership has recently apologized for earlier practices of racial segregation, and the denomination has recently elected a Black president, Southern Baptists remain predominantly white and extremely conservative on social issues. (While the SBC had originally taken a moderate position on abortion, the 1979 upheaval resulted in a rapid and complete reversal, following the lead of the emergent Moral Majority in seizing on this as a wedge issue.)

After gaining membership rapidly during the late twentieth century, Southern Baptist membership – together with that of other Evangelical/Fundamentalist churches – began to tend downward because of sex scandals involving powerful leaders; a growing disinterest in organized religion among younger people; and a rejection by many of Culture Wars crusading. The ongoing Fundamentalist takeover of the SBC in the 1980s, for example, resulted in a major upheaval at Southeastern Baptist Seminary in North Carolina, and the subsequent establishment at nearby Wake Forest University of the Wake Forest School of Divinity, an ecumenical institution that identifies with the Baptist tradition. Similarly, lifelong Baptist Jimmy Carter convened in 2007 the New Baptist Covenant, an association of Southern Baptist congregations that repudiated the SBC fundamentalist reorientation.

In addition to the SBC, a considerable number of very conservative Baptist churches identify as Independent Baptists, rejecting the national organizational structure of the SBC as too compromising of congregational autonomy.

An important subset of Evangelicalism is known as fundamentalism. Religious Right leader Jerry Falwell once defined a fundamentalist (himself included) as an Evangelical who was angry about something. Fundamentalism is a loosely organized and defined movement within the Evangelical community that arose in the late nineteenth century as a conservative response to the implications of German biblical criticism and Darwinian evolution for a literal interpretation of Hebrew and Christian Scripture. By the early twentieth century it had solidified into an organized movement, promoted by a series of books known as The Fundamentals. In addition to the tenets of Evangelicalism, Fundamentalists formulated Five Points which they believed essential for true Christian belief, all based on the notion that Scripture is infallible and must be interpreted literally. (The Authorized, or King James, version of the Bible of 1611 is the preferred English translation.) These points include the Virgin Birth and bodily Resurrection of Jesus, the authenticity of Jesus's miracles, and the Substitutionary Atonement (Jesus's death for the redemption of sinners). Splits within the Baptist and Presbyterian communities resulted in this firm drawing of theological battle lines.

Following the major setback of the 1925 Scopes Trial, fundamentalism continued to flourish quietly, particularly in the South, and developed a network of churches, Sunday schools, Bible colleges, summer camps, periodicals, and radio stations. These promoted their cause in a decentralized but effective fashion. Billy Graham, as noted, gave the movement national visibility beginning in the 1950s and helped the movement make strategic accommodations with contemporary American middle-class culture in order to promote the message more effectively.

Following the public relations successes of Billy Graham and Jimmy Carter – neither of whom in their later careers would have accepted the fundamentalist label – Carter's disappointment of right-wing Evangelicals by his moderate policies during his presidency led quickly to a fundamentalist backlash. By the late 1970s, ambitious preachers such as Jerry Falwell Sr. and Pat Robertson set about organizing the "Moral Majority" movement, seeking support from conservative Catholics and Jews as well as fellow Evangelicals. The movement was openly political, and turned against Carter to help elect Ronald Reagan as President in 1980. (Reagan was not a frequent churchgoer, but publicly welcomed Moral Majority support.)

The Moral Majority and similar evangelically aligned conservative movements employed grassroots organizing, lobbying, direct mailing, and, perhaps most importantly, the use of electronic media such as radio, television, and, later, the Internet. Fox News and the conservative shift in both the Southern Baptist Convention and the Republican Party turned the movement into a powerful force in aligning religion and politics in a drive to bring about a realignment in American culture. These forces utilized a number of real or imaginary issues and foes to rally support: evolution, prayer in public schools, Communism, socialism, "secular humanism," abortion, gay rights, transsexualism, feminism and, in recent years, Critical Race Theory. By the time of the 2016 presidential election, a large majority of Evangelicals had aligned themselves with Donald Trump, and the lines between politics and religion had become blurry.

Scripture and Holidays

Most Baptists recognize major Christian holidays such as Christmas and Easter. Different versions of the Bible may be found across the spectrum. Traditionalists sometimes favor the King James (Authorized) Version, which translates certain key words more in accordance with conservative teachings. Worship follows the Reformed pattern, with particular stress on preaching. Baptism, a key practice, is by immersion for adult believers.

Culturally Responsive Pedagogy

The prominence of Baptists in recent political controversies suggests that a discussion of the relationship between religion and politics on the American scene could be illuminating, if handled very carefully.

Common Misunderstandings

As should be evident from the historical background above, Baptists come in all shapes and sizes from the moderate American Baptists to the heavily fundamentalist Southern Baptist

Convention. Non-Baptists may mischaracterize all Baptists as fundamentalists, and the distinctions among Baptists should be pointed out when appropriate.

Notes

1 Source: https://en.wikipedia.org/wiki/American_Baptist_Churches_USA.
2 https://en.wikipedia.org/wiki/Southern_Baptist_Convention.

Further Reading and Resources

"Baptists Explained." https://www.youtube.com/watch?v=Zcc5QuQ6RXY
Lippy, Charles H., and Peter W. Williams, eds. *Encyclopedia of Religion in America*. Washington, DC: CQ Press, 2010, "Baptists: African American," (I, 224–229); "Baptist Denominations," (I, 230–237); "Baptists: Southern," (I, 246–253); "Baptists: Tradition and Heritage," (I, 254–267).
"Southern Baptist Worship Service." https://www.youtube.com/watch?v=2n-5dxknkEk
"Sunday Worship Service…First Baptist Church, West Hartford." https://www.youtube.com/watch?v=oTUaC9Kw3ec

12

Christianity: Black Churches

> Sometimes referred to as "The Black National Anthem," "Lift Ev'ry Voice and Sing" is a hymn widely known and sung in African American churches. The lyrics were written in 1900 by the famous African American poet James Weldon Johnson and the music was composed by his brother J. Rosamond Johnson. Drawing on themes from the Book of Exodus, the song reflects on the painful history of enslavement and exhorts the people to remember God's role in their emancipation and to continue to hope and work for full liberation.
>
> This song has long been a unifying religious and cultural artifact, known and sung across the diverse array of African American churches as well as in many majority-African American schools. It has recently enjoyed a resurgence, sung in protests and marches in the wake of the 2020 murder by police of George Floyd, and incorporated into major national sporting events such as the Super Bowl.

Membership

Accurate information on Black church membership has been historically difficult to pinpoint. Pew Research reports the following for 2021–2022:

> In the current survey, 23% of Black Protestants identify with one of the eight historically Black Protestant

DOI: 10.4324/9781003405894-12

denominations that make up the *Conference of National Black Churches*. This includes 9% who identify with the National Baptist Convention, USA (or simply with the "National Baptist Convention"), 6% who identify with the Church of God in Christ (COGIC), 3% who identify with the African Methodist Episcopal Church, and 2% who identify with the National Baptist Convention of America. The Progressive National Baptist Convention, African Methodist Episcopal Zion Church, and Christian Methodist Episcopal Church are each the denominational homes for 1% of Black Protestants in the survey; fewer than 1% of Black Protestants surveyed identify as Full Gospel Baptists.[1]

The roughly 75% of African Americans who do not formally identify as members of these denominations include Roman Catholics (many originally from Maryland and Louisiana, sites of early Catholic settlement), Jehovah's Witnesses, Nation of Islam and other Muslims, nondenominational Christians, members of independent churches, etc. In short, African Americans are far from being religiously homogeneous.

Historical Overview

Although all Mainline denominations welcome African Americans and members of other minority groups, 11 o'clock Sunday morning remains, in the phrase of Martin Luther King Jr., "the most segregated hour of Christian America." That many Black Christians worship separately from their White counterparts is certainly true, but its explanation is more complicated than simply the reality of White-imposed racial segregation.

In the days of slavery prior to the Civil War, enslaved Blacks in the South were often compelled to attend White-led services, either in all-Black congregations or in the rear or the balconies of White churches. Many also met surreptitiously in "hush harbors," secluded rural sites where they could practice an African-influenced form of worship without White supervision.

In the North and, after the Civil War, in the South, free Blacks were usually unwelcome at White churches and began to form their own denominations, usually Baptist or Methodist. As a result, the African Methodist Episcopal Church (AME), AME Zion Church, and a variety of groups using variations of the term National Baptist had come into being by the early twentieth century.

As the Holiness and Pentecostal movements began to spread through the South and the industrial cities of the Great Lakes to which many Blacks had migrated to escape the repressive sharecropper system, many African Americans adopted their ways. These resonated with their highly expressive approach to worship, which fitted well with that of slavery days. Pentecostals focused on the experience of the Holy Spirit descending upon them, expressed through speaking in tongues, ecstatic dancing, and uninhibited Gospel music which both influenced and was in turn influenced by White Gospel. (Elvis Presley is a good example of this cultural crossover.)

Meeting places for Black congregations varied mainly according to social and economic status. Poor inner-city churches often worshiped in rented storefronts, while their rural counterparts built modest wooden structures in the fields. More prosperous urban Baptists and Methodists were able to build substantial Gothic and Romanesque churches in Black neighborhoods, which often became a major focus of communal life. Still later, Prosperity Gospel preachers were able to attract sufficient followings to erect megachurches, sometime racially integrated.

The Black Church dramatically became the focus not only of African American but of American life more broadly during the 1950s and 60s, as the campaign for civil rights, led in good part by clergy such as Martin Luther King Jr. and Ralph Abernathy, resulted in a revolution of Black empowerment. Before his assassination, though, King began to turn his attention toward the war in Vietnam and other issues. After his death, his movement began to splinter, with more secular groups such as the Black Panthers and new religious movements such as the Nation of Islam (Black Muslims) vying for leadership within the African American community.

In the present time, Sunday morning is still a largely segregated time, but now more by free choice rather than compulsion. The Black Church has traditionally been a unifying institution within its community, and clergy have often played civic as well as religious leadership roles. Although African Americans are now welcomed in many predominantly White Mainline congregations, Black worship continues to serve as a focal point for communal self-understanding and cultural preservation.

Scripture and Holidays

African American worship and religious life more generally is steeped in Hebrew and Christian scripture, as illustrated in Martin Luther King Jr.'s sermons. Worship is more free-flowing and participatory than in most predominantly White churches, and Black Gospel music is a distinctive characteristic of such worship. Sermons are lengthy and melodious, often sounding more like chanting than speaking. Music is drawn from, among other sources, a rich tradition of Negro spirituals and Black gospel hymns. There are no standard Bible translations.

Culturally Responsive Pedagogy

Listen to sermons by Rev. Dr. Martin Luther King, Jr.; Reverend Ike (Frederick J. Eikerenkoetter II); Rev. Dr. Jacquelyn Grant; and Bishop T.D. Jakes. How are they similar and different?

Find out whether your community was involved in the Civil Rights movement. Were local churches involved?

Note

1   Source: https://www.pewresearch.org/religion/2021/02/16/religious-affiliation-and-congregations/.

Further Reading and Resources

"Faith and Religion among Black Americans." https://www.pewresearch.org/religion/2021/02/16/faith-among-black-americans/

Lippy, Charles H., and Peter W. Williams, eds. *Encyclopedia of Religion in America*. Washington, DC: CQ Press, 2010, "African American Religion: Colonial Era through the Civil War," (I, 33–42), "African-American Religion: From the Civil War to Civil Rights" (I, 43–50), and "African-American Religion: Post-Civil Rights Era" (I, 43–50).

"The Black Church: Gospel Music and the Civil Rights Movement." https://www.youtube.com/watch?v=dGxiQMLVYss&list=PLzkQfVIJun2Ig PF38yicxUTADK6iXwmjm (and others in the PBS series "The Black Church: Inside look").

"The Black Church." https://www.pbs.org/wgbh/americanexperience/features/godinamerica-black-church/

"Exploring Faith and the Black Church." https://www.pewtrusts.org/en/trust/archive/fall-2021/exploring-faith-and-black-churches-in-america

13

Christianity: Christian Science

> In 1908 Mary Baker Eddy, the founder of the Christian Science movement, established a newspaper, *The Christian Science Monitor*, in order to combat what she regarded as unfair and untruthful reporting about the movement in other newspapers. The *Monitor* over the years established itself as an accurate and respected publication, distancing itself from Eddy's concerns as her aegis faded. In recent years, in response to the decline of print journalism, it has gone electronic, billing itself as the *CS Monitor* or just the *Monitor*, though it has not abandoned its original name. The shift may be mainly a marketing ploy similar to Colonel Sanders's Kentucky Fried Chicken being abbreviated to KFC, but also perhaps a sign of the distancing of the newspaper's identity from its sectarian origins and purposes.

Introduction

The church estimates that world membership comes to about 400,000. Non-church sources estimate membership at around 100,000.[1]

Historical Overview

Mary Baker Eddy was born in New Hampshire in 1821. In her youth, she suffered from chronic invalidism until finding relief through the work of Phineas P. Quimby, a clockmaker and student of mesmerism (hypnosis) who taught that disease was illusory and curable by correcting the mental errors that were its cause. In 1866 she experienced a fall from which she recovered by reading a biblical account of Jesus healing the sick. She soon went on to develop the theory that Jesus's message was essentially about the healing power of the divine mind, and that she had discovered the scientific basis underlying Christianity. Eddy's system rejected the Christian idea of the Trinity and maintained that God was a principle rather than a person and that Jesus was a "way-shower" rather than a divinity. God had both male and female aspects, and women played a leading role in the organization from its beginnings.

She expounded that message in 1875 in her book, *Science and Health and Key to the Scriptures*, and soon founded an organization into an organization in 1879 that expanded rapidly and underwent a number of name changes. The imposing Mother Church in Boston was erected in 1894, and remains the center of the denomination. In its early years, Christian Science achieved success in part through the unreliability of professional medicine during the Victorian era and appealed especially to women who, like Eddy, found themselves transplanted from small towns to anonymous cities such as Boston. Other religious movements based on "metaphysics" such as New Thought also emerged during the early twentieth century, but Eddy vigorously repudiated them. The organization grew rapidly until the 1930s, then went into a decline that has continued till the present, presumably in part due to the vast improvements in scientific medicine taking place in the twentieth century and the growing familiarity of Americans with urban life.

Scriptures, Worship, and Holidays

Christian Science regards two texts as inspired: *The Bible* and *Science and Health*. Worship is held in churches and conducted by two readers, each reading from one of these texts. Wednesday evening services consist of testimonials by members as to healings they have experienced. There are no ordained clergy, but "practitioners" may be licensed and charged for prayer. Prayer is individualistic, and consists of private meditation in which believers struggle to free themselves from the bonds of materialist thought. The denomination maintains reading rooms in many cities in which visitors or believers may quietly peruse Scientist literature.

Common Misunderstandings, Stereotypes, and Classroom Concerns

Christian Science, a force on the American religious scene a century ago, has so diminished in numbers and influence that few students are likely to be aware of its existence except in major urban centers, especially Boston. Much of its appeal was replaced by that of the "New Age" movement that emerged in the 1970s, which focused on personal transformation outside institutional bounds. Court cases involving the liability of parents who denied medical treatment for their children are no longer an issue. Should the topic arise, providing clear information about its character seems like the best means of dispelling misinformation.

Note

1 Valente, Judy, "Christian Science Healing," *PBS*. August 1, 2008.

Further Reading and Resources

Christian Science Committee on Institutional Work in California. "What Christian Scientists Believe." 2013. https://www.youtube.com/watch?v=tJYLWHMpFlE.

Lippy, Charles H., and Peter Williams, eds. *Encyclopedia of Religion in America*. Washington DC: CQ Press, 2010, "Christian Science" (I, 440–448).

14

Christianity: Jehovah's Witnesses

> Jehovah's Witnesses believe that it is incumbent upon them to spread their message from door to door. For many Americans, this aggressive evangelization constitutes a violation of their privacy, but to Jehovah's Witnesses this is an important part of their faith.

Introduction

U.S. Membership: 1,233,000 (early 2020s)[1]

Historical Overview

Jehovah's Witnesses originated in the late 1870s and were originally known as the Bible Student movement. They expect the second coming of Jesus to be imminent. After this second coming Jesus will inaugurate God's government on earth. Witnesses differ from more traditional Christians in their rejection of the Trinity, among other teachings. They are known for their door-to-door evangelization.

Common Misunderstandings, Stereotypes, and Classroom Concerns

In the public school context, the Witnesses reject the Flag Salute, the singing of the national anthem, and other manifestations of patriotic observance. They also refuse military service. Their right to exempt their children from such practices has been upheld by the Supreme Court. They also reject the observance of Christmas, Easter, and other holidays, as well as that of birthdays. This latter prohibition may vary from family to family, and some teacher-parent negotiations may be necessary to establish boundaries. Blood transfusions are prohibited, which could lead to some difficult situations if a student is injured seriously. Although Witnesses at one time rejected compulsory vaccination, this is no longer an issue.

Culturally Responsive Pedagogy

The Witnesses, once dismissed as a "cult" (no longer an acceptable term for religious scholars), are definitely outsiders on the spectrum of American Christianity. Their door-to-door evangelism, like that of Mormons, makes them widely known. Their millennialism and their distinctive interpretation of certain scriptural passages could make for an interesting, if carefully managed, discussion of such themes.

Note

1   Source: https://www.jw.org/en/jehovahs-witnesses/worldwide/US/.

Further Reading and Resources

"Jehovah's Witnesses Explained." https://www.youtube.com/watch?v=ED1EtSz9Beshttps://www.youtube.com/watch?v=ED1EtSz9Bes

Lippy, Charles H., and Peter W. Williams, eds. *Encyclopedia of Religion in America*. Washington, DC: CQ Press, 2010, "Jehovah's Witnesses" (II, 1106–1108).

15

Christianity: Latter-Day Saints

> The popular musical "The Book of Mormon" is an affectionate satire more on popular conceptions of Mormonism than on Mormons and their religion themselves. The central theme of the show is the Mormon practice of sending out young people – girls as well as boys – on two-year mission trips throughout the United States and much of the rest of the world, in those places that are legal and safe for them to go. Even though their success rate in making converts is not always as high as they might hope, the experience is a rite of passage that promotes maturity and continued commitment to their religion.

Introduction

U.S. Membership: 6,868,793 (2024)[1]

Historical Overview

The Latter-day Saints – familiarly known as Mormons – originated from the revelations and leadership of Joseph Smith in western New York in the 1820s. Smith claimed that he had been granted supernatural access by the Archangel Moroni to a set of gold plates that revealed the coming of Jesus to the New World and beginning a new movement, the adherents of which were eventually defeated by enemies and disappeared into history. This story was recounted in the golden plates and, translated by Smith, became the distinctive sacred narrative of the movement – *The Book of Mormon* – in addition to Hebrew and Christian scriptures.

Smith gathered adherents who moved first to Ohio, then Missouri, and finally to Nauvoo, Illinois, where Smith was assassinated. The main band of these "Mormons" followed Smith's successor, Brigham Young, to the Utah Territory, where they established a thriving society in Salt Lake City, still the movement's headquarters. There, they created and maintained a distinctive culture with a distinctive form of worship, an intense work ethic, healthy living – no alcohol, caffeine, or tobacco – and a strong system of mutual support.

The Saints remained at odds with the dominant society for some time over the issue of plural marriage, which they finally ended in 1890 in order to permit the new state of Utah to enter the Union. During the twentieth century the Mormons, while retaining their base in Utah and contiguous states, have expanded throughout the nation and evangelized widely abroad. Pairs of young missionaries spend two years on missions, most of them overseas, seeking converts and thereby reinforcing a strong sense of group identity.

Scripture and Holidays

The *Book of Mormon* and two supplementary texts – *Doctrine and Covenants* and *Pearl of Great Price* – revealed to Joseph Smith, together with the Hebrew and Christian scriptures, remain foundational to Mormon belief and practice.

Sunday worship consists of an hour-long service held in the chapel within a meetinghouse. The service, called the "sacrament meeting," lasts an hour and consists of prayers and sermons offered by members of the congregation, the singing of hymns both broadly Christian and specifically Mormon, and the receipt of the sacrament consisting of bread and water.

While Sunday service in chapels is open to all, only members are able to attend temple rituals. (When new temples are opened, which is frequently, outsiders – "gentiles" in Mormon parlance – are welcomed for a brief period.) Temples are larger and more elaborate than meetinghouses, and often boast a distinctive design. The Salt Lake City Temple is the most prominent, with some 200 in active operation throughout the world. Temples are utilized for endowment ceremonies, in which members are initiated through rituals into full status in the church and are given passwords and temple garments and enter into covenants assuring their status in the present and future. Mormons also maintain extensive genealogical resources through which non-LDS ancestors may be baptized into the church.

Common Misunderstandings and Classroom Concerns

As Mormons have become prosperous and better integrated into American society, their presence is distinctive but no longer perceived by most as threatening. The notoriety created by their practice of polygamy (plural marriage) during their early history has long since been renounced, although it can still be found in some break-off groups in the American Southwest and in Mexico. They tend to be conservative both in politics and lifestyle. The 2012 presidential candidacy of Mitt Romney, though unsuccessful, raised the Mormon community into public prominence, and presumably put to rest any lingering impression of Mormons as not quite fully American. Mormon children usually attend public schools, and their presence seldom raises any difficulties.

Culturally Responsive Pedagogy

Other than in Utah and contiguous states, as well as larger metropolitan areas, many students may find Mormonism exotic, mysterious, and even dangerous. Local resource persons and videos may be helpful to present them simply as ordinary Americans with some distinctive beliefs and practices.

Note

1 Church of Jesus Christ of Latter-Day Saints, Facts and Statistics, https://newsroom.churchofjesuschrist.org/facts-and-statistics/country/united-states.

Further Reading and Resources

"Latter-day Saints Temples." https://www.youtube.com/watch?v=ejf9a70qgI8

Lippy, Charles H., and Peter W. Williams, eds. *Encyclopedia of Religion in America*. Washington, DC: CQ Press, 2010, "Latter-day Saints" (III, 1214–1220).

"What Is Mormonism? What Do Mormons Believe?" https://www.youtube.com/watch?v=CeaC6NnhyIE

"What to Expect at Church Services." https://www.youtube.com/watch?v=JaMgGaRxhJ0

16

Christianity: Lutherans

> An old joke that explains the differences among different groups of American Lutherans involves four Lutherans – two men and two women – and a car. In the first scenario, two men wearing clerical collars are in the front seat, with one driving, with the women in the back seat. That's the Missouri Synod. In take two, the men are in the front seat and the women are behind, pushing the car. That's the Wisconsin Synod. In the final vignette, both the women and the men are wearing collars and arguing about who gets to drive the car. That's the Evangelical Lutheran Church in America (ELCA).

Introduction

Membership Statistics

- U.S. membership of ELCA (Evangelical Lutheran Church in America) 2,904, 686 (2022)[1]
- U.S. membership of Lutheran Church – Missouri Synod 1,545,124 (2018)[2]
- Lutheran Church – Wisconsin Synod 335,879 (2022)[3]

Historical Overview

The term *Protestant* originated in the 1520s as German princes supporting Martin Luther protested attempts by the Catholic Church to suppress his teachings. Luther, a German monk turned reformer, objected initially to the sale of indulgences, a guarantee of a reduced term in *Purgatory* after death, to finance the building of a new St. Peter's Cathedral by the Pope in Rome. Luther's 95 Theses of 1517 launched an even broader critique of the supremacy of the Pope over the entirety of Christianity, which for Luther had compromised the ultimate authority of the Bible. Luther further objected to the notion that salvation could be obtained by "works righteousness" – observing Church ordinances and performing good works – rather than by faith bestowed on the individual directly by God's grace. This trio of salvation through grace, faith, and Scripture became central not only to Luther's followers, but to the broader movement that came to be known as *Protestantism*. To further his emphasis on Scripture, Luther translated the entirety of the Bible from Hebrew and Greek into a new synthesis of German which he derived from the multitude of dialects accessible to him to enable biblical literacy among lay people as well as Latin-reading clergy.

Protestantism was never a unified movement, but it rapidly spread in Luther's day as it became linked with efforts by civil rulers to break free of the control of the Pope and the Holy Roman Empire. Germany at the time was not yet a nation but rather a loose aggregate of dozens of larger and small political units speaking various dialects of a shared language. In this context princes eager to throw off Roman control seized on Luther's movement as a rationale for political self-assertion. Although parts of Germany remained Catholic and still others adopted different versions of the Protestant movement, much of what is now Germany followed Luther. Eventually, *Lutheranism* – Luther would not have been happy with that term since he saw himself as restoring biblical Christianity – spread into most of Scandinavia, and by the eighteenth century followed lines on immigration into the American colonies and subsequent nation.

Lutherans are those who follow the movement begun by Martin Luther in the early 1500 in Saxony. In the United States, they settled first in Pennsylvania, then followed lines of German and Scandinavian immigration into the Midwest. Many of these Lutherans practiced episcopal polity – governance by bishops – but lacked any central organization. Each ethnic group created its own *synods* – regional associations similar to dioceses – which by the early twentieth century had begun to outlive their usefulness as subsequent generations became English-speaking. Smaller synods consolidated into two large, aggregated denominations – the American Lutheran Church and the Lutheran Church in America – which merged in 1988 to form today's *Evangelical Lutheran Church in America (ELCA).* (The term "Evangelical" – from the Greek word for "gospel" – here is a historical reference to Martin Luther's use of the word to refer to the biblical basis of faith.) Another smaller Lutheran group that has resisted merger into the ELCA is the *Missouri Synod*, which leans toward a Fundamentalist approach to biblical interpretation and theology. Even smaller – and more conservative groups – such as the *Wisconsin Synod* have also maintained their independence from the Mainline.

Scriptures and Holidays

ELCA Lutheran churches today are very much part of the "Mainline," and utilize a liturgy very similar to that of Episcopalians and Roman Catholics. They retain an ethnic base – German and Scandinavian – larger than that of other Mainline denominations, and maintain some food and other folkways more as nostalgia than as having any particular religious significance.

Most Lutherans follow the three-year liturgical calendar of Scripture readings utilized by Roman Catholics and Mainline Protestant denominations, as well as the *New Revised Standard* and other contemporary biblical translations. (*Die Luther Bibel* occupies the same place in Lutheran practice as does the *King James Version* for Episcopalians, a beloved but rather archaic artifact.)

Common Misunderstandings

Although most North American Lutheran churches originated as German or Scandinavian ethnic churches, the vast majority today consist of highly assimilated middle-class Americans. Thus, old in-group jokes about, say, Swedish Lutherans making fun of Norwegians are now more folkloric than immediately relevant.

Culturally Responsive Pedagogy

In parts of Pennsylvania and the Midwest, Lutheran students may be willing and able to share stories about old Lutheran customs and traditions.

For Discussion: Why are there so many different Lutheran denominations? What does this tell us more generally about religion in the United States?

Notes

1 Evangelical Lutheran Church in America, About the ELCA, https://www.elca.org/about.
2 The Lutheran Church-Missouri Synod, Rosters and Statistics, https://files.lcms.org/file/preview/0P6YfWqhIvpvei9cTSh0dBsbgoWy78VV.
3 Wisconsin Evangelical Lutheran Synod, About WELS, https://wels.net/about-wels/.

Further Reading and Resources

"An Outsider Visits a [Missouri Synod] Lutheran Church." https://www.youtube.com/watch?v=99fmOmIcF0c

ELCA website. https://en.wikipedia.org/wiki/Evangelical_Lutheran_Church_in_America

Lippy, Charles H., and Peter W. Williams, eds. *Encyclopedia of Religion in America*. Washington, DC: CQ Press, 2010, "Lutheran Churches" (III, 1289–1297) and "Lutheran Tradition and Heritage" (III, 1298–1308).

"Lutheran Worship: Introduction." https://www.youtube.com/watch?v=hAuAuxg2Sp4

Missouri Synod website. https://www.lcms.org/about (denominational website).

"Understanding Lutheranism." https://www.youtube.com/watch?v=EWl239CklOY

Wisconsin Synod website. https://wels.net/

17

Christianity: Methodist, Moravian, Wesleyan, and Holiness Churches

> In the evening [of May 12, 1738] I went very unwillingly to a [Moravian] society on Aldersgate Street [in London], where one was reading Luther's preface to the Epistle to the Romans. About a quarter before nine, while he was describing the change which God works in the heart through faith in Christ, I felt my heart strangely warmed.
> *Journal of John Wesley*

Introduction

Membership Statistics

U.S. United Methodist Church Membership Statistics: 5,424,175 (2024)[1]

U.S. Moravian Church: about 40,000 (2023)[2]

Historical Overview

The Methodist tradition dates back to the University of Oxford in mid-eighteenth-century England, where the brothers John and Charles Wesley – later to become priests in the Church of England – participated in a "Holy Club" aimed at fostering the systematic pursuit of piety, as well as social service such as visiting prisoners, among their fellow students. John served briefly and not very successfully as a missionary in Georgia, and soon after his return to England experienced a religious conversion which he described as having had his heart "strangely warmed." (See anecdote above.)

The Wesley brothers banded together to help organize lay-led groups within the Church of England that would supplement, though not replace, what they regarded as the overly formal Anglican worship of the day. (The name "Methodist" describes John's tightly controlled or "methodical" system of organization and practice.) Charles became known particularly as a prolific hymn-writer, and many of his approximately 6,500 compositions are still sung today. ("Hark, the Herald Angels Sing" is probably his best-known composition.)

Although the Wesley brothers never separated from the Church of England, their American followers did so at the time of Independence. At the "Christmas Conference" of 1784, dozens of Methodist preachers, mainly from the New York and Baltimore areas, convened in the latter city to organize an independent *Methodist Episcopal Church* with Francis Asbury and Thomas Coke as its first bishops. (The term "Episcopal," now rarely utilized by the mainline United Methodist Church, refers to a polity utilizing bishops as regional overseers.) The Methodist (or Wesleyan) movement rapidly spread through the South especially through the use of circuit riders, unmarried young men on horseback who rode tirelessly around carefully planned routes, preaching the word until settlements grew large enough to plant permanent churches with a settled, educated ministry.

In the 1840s, Methodists, like Baptists and Presbyterians, split regionally over the issue of slavery, and did not reunite until

1939. A 1968 merger brought the reunited denomination into union with the *Evangelical United Brethren,* a group of German origin that shared Wesleyan principles, to form today's *United Methodist Church.* By the early 2020s, the latter stood again on the brink of division over the issues of same-sex marriage and ordination, with opposition to those practices coming in part from the UMC's considerable overseas membership, especially in Africa.

Both the Holiness and Pentecostal movements have their origins in the Methodist/Wesleyan traditions. *Holiness* emerged as a distinctive denominational cluster in the Northeast and Midwest during the later nineteenth century in protest against what its followers perceived as the "worldliness" of Mainline Methodists, many of whom were rapidly becoming assimilated into middle-class American society. Early Holiness followers rejected "worldly" artifacts and practices such as neckties, bobbed hair, and movies as well as long-established Methodist bans on alcohol and tobacco. They soon coalesced into denominations, which often fractured and then reconfigured themselves, such as the Church of God (Anderson, Indiana) and the Church of the Nazarene. In recent decades, Holiness denominations have entered more into the cultural mainstream, and their practices and megachurch worship spaces are similar to those of other Evangelicals. Like contemporary Pentecostals, they tend to embrace the political views of the Religious Right.

In addition to the UMC, smaller Methodist denominations also exist, including three with predominantly Black membership discussed in the entry on Black churches.

The Moravian Church has close historical affinities with Methodism, and today is in full communion with the United Methodist Church as well as The Episcopal Church, the ELCA Lutheran church, and a variety of small denominations that share their governance by bishops. The group in its modern incarnation originated in the 1720s in what is now the Czech Republic under the leadership of Count Ludwig von Zinzendorf. This movement was a manifestation of German *pietism,* but featuring a distinctive emotional devotion to the wounds of Jesus. Moravians soon began to send missionaries to the North

American colonies, especially aimed at Native Americans. They established communitarian settlements in Bethlehem PA and (Winston-) Salem NC, which remain the centers of their northern and southern branches in the United States. They stress piety, pacificism, evangelism, liturgical worship, and ecumenism, and maintain a rich and distinctive musical tradition.

Scripture and Holidays

Methodist worship and use of scripture are similar to other mainline groups, although more influenced by Anglican/Episcopal practice than others more squarely in the Reformed lineage. The prolific production of hymns by co-founder Charles Wesley has left an understandable impact on Methodists as well as other denominations.

Common Misunderstandings, Stereotypes, and Classroom Concerns

Methodists are one of the largest and most widely distributed American religious groups, and practice a lifestyle no longer any different from other "mainline" denominations. Moravians are not well known outside of some regions of North Carolina and Pennsylvania, and few students have probably ever heard of them.

Culturally Responsive Pedagogy

To elicit discussion on Methodism, questions such as the following might be asked:

1. The United Methodist Church has a large membership not only in the United States but also in other parts of the world as well. What might this have to do with the denomination's facing a major split in the 2020s?

2. Listen to the selections of Methodist and Moravian hymns on the YouTube videos listed below. What might they tell us about the piety of the two related denominations?

Notes

1   Source: https://www.umdata.org/statistics.
2   Source: https://www.moravian.org/2018/07/quick-facts-about-the-moravian-church/.

Further Reading and Resources

Lippy, Charles H., and Peter W. Williams, eds. *Encyclopedia of Religion in America*. Washington, DC: CQ Press, 2010, "Methodists: Through the Nineteenth Century" (III, 1346–1353), "Methodists: Since the Nineteenth Century" (III, 1354–1361), "Methodists: Tradition and Heritage" (III, 1362–1374), "Moravians" (III, 1427–1431).

"Methodist Hymns." https://www.youtube.com/playlist?list=PL9MobCMJBbT_1cq6uZVopmUZz7LuAOAh6

18

Christianity: Orthodox

> The Russian Revolution of 1917 included a systematic campaign against the Russian Orthodox Church, since the church and the Czarist regime were closely entangled and many church leaders were subsequently killed as enemies of the Revolution. St. Nicholas Cathedral in Washington DC was built in 1930 as a National War Memorial Shrine honoring, among many others, the Holy New Martyrs and Confessors of Russia. Among these were the "Royal Passion Bearers," Czar Nicholas II and his family. In the early 1990s Russian iconographers designed and executed iconography in the Russo-Byzantine style of the 12th century commemorating and sanctifying the association of church and state in the czarist era, and how that memory has continued to pervade the lives of their spiritual successors in the New World. The shrine illustrates how closely religion, politics, and ethnic identity have been associated in even recent history in the story of Orthodoxy, even as the Orthodox Church of America has worked to separate ethnicity from faith.

Introduction

Statistics

U.S. Membership: 675,000 (2020)[1]
Oriental Orthodox 491,913

Source:https://orthodoxreality.org/wp-content/uploads/2021/03/2020CensusGeneralReport1.pdf

Historical Overview

Eastern Orthodoxy is among the oldest varieties of Christianity, having originated in the Roman Empire in the earliest days of the new Christian religion. Until the Emperor Constantine's move of the capital of the Empire from Rome to Byzantium in 324 – after which it acquired the name Constantinople – there had been no clear division of Christianity into factions competing for primacy, but rather a number of ancient cities in the Mediterranean basin in which centers of religious authority emerged: Alexandria, Antioch, Jerusalem, Rome and, eventually, Constantinople. With Constantine's removal of his capital eastward, however, Rome was left isolated in the western portion of a now splintered empire, and its bishop – the Pope – was left not only to provide religious leadership in the Latin-speaking portion of that empire, but also to maintain a civil government and military as well.

Back in the Greek-speaking East, however, the leaders of Christianity – bishops – were forced to acknowledge the authority of an Emperor who had himself become a Christian, and who did not hesitate to use his authority to intervene in religious matters. The Christianity that henceforth developed in the East was barred from extensive involvement with political matters, and instead focused on worship focused on mysteries (similar to Roman Catholic sacraments) – rituals providing access to divine saving grace – and on icons, sacred images of Jesus and the saints that adorn the interiors of churches and are believed to afford access to the supernatural realm and unity with God. The theology of Orthodoxy was thus mystical in emphasis, centered on the process of the believer becoming increasingly godlike through communal worship.

The eastern and western regions of the empire became isolated and estranged during the following centuries, culminating in the Great Schism of 1054 in which the Archbishop of Rome – the Pope – and the Patriarch of Constantinople, the first among equals of the Eastern archbishops, mutually excommunicated one another in a division that even today has never fully healed. In our narrative, what came to be known as Eastern Orthodoxy enters with the "New Immigration" to the United States following the Civil War, in this case from Russia, Greece, Romania, Bulgaria, Ukraine, Serbia, and parts of the Balkans and the Middle East. Many of these traditionally Orthodox immigrants settled in the mining and manufacturing areas of the Great Lakes region, where new industries – steel and auto-making – required vast amounts of unskilled labor. As soon as they were able to afford to, these immigrants began to erect churches with their traditional onion-shaped domes in the coal fields of western Pennsylvania and working-class ethnic neighborhoods of Pittsburgh, Cleveland, Detroit, Chicago, Milwaukee, and smaller cities where immigrant labor was concentrated. An even earlier stream of Orthodox migration followed the Russian settlement of Alaska in the late eighteenth century, from which the tradition and its missionary clergy spread southward into California and beyond.

Eastern Orthodoxy in the New World remained segregated by ethnicity as long as Old World divisions and languages shaped religious consciousness and traditional regional cultures still resisted assimilation into the broader American melting pot. By 1963, however, such ancient distinctions had begun to erode sufficiently that the Orthodox Church in America (OCA) parted ways with Russian Orthodoxy to provide a pan-ethnic, English-speaking version of Orthodoxy for Americans of various ethnic backgrounds, including those who had embraced Orthodoxy by marriage or conversion from other Christian groups. The older ethnic-based churches have by no means disappeared, but their power continues to wane along with that of their traditional constituencies.

Scripture and Holidays

There is no official translation of Scripture in English, although the Orthodox Study Bible is recommended by many. The Orthodox version, like the Roman Catholic, includes the Deuterocanonical books (the Apocrypha), which come between the Hebrew and Christian scriptures but are rejected by most Protestant churches.

Orthodox worship usually takes place in churches with domes: rounded domes in Greek tradition, "onion (pointed) domes" in Russian. Orthodox in America use the traditional Divine Liturgy of St. John Chrysostom. Icons – images of Jesus and the saints – play a major part in Orthodox church decoration, lining the walls, the altar screen (iconostasis), and the dome. Icons, with stylized images and gold background, are believed to be vehicles through which the earthly and supernatural realms intersect. Only the priest and his assistants are permitted behind the altar screen, which is closed during the consecration of the elements. Priests are permitted to marry before consecration, but not afterward.

(See the following unit for holidays.)

Common Misunderstandings, Stereotypes, and Classroom Concerns

One conspicuous difference between the Orthodox churches and other branches of American Christianity is the date for the celebration of Easter, which usually takes place a week or more later than that observed by Roman Catholics and others. (This difference originated in Pope Gregory XIII's calendar reform of 1582, which displaced the older Julian calendar dating back to the time of the Roman Empire.) Since the celebration of Easter primarily involves Sunday, no difficulties for schools or governmental institutions are involved. Colorful customs such as painted Easter eggs may be found in Orthodox ethnic neighborhoods, but seldom evoke any controversy. The Orthodox faith, in short, is readily compatible with American laws and institutions.

One thing non-Orthodox students may find confusing is the distinction between Orthodox churches and Eastern-rite (Byzantine) Catholic churches. A tour of an Orthodox church, even virtually (see resources below), can be eye-opening.

Note

1 Orthodox Christian Laity, "Eastern Orthodoxy Gains New Followers in America," https://ocl.org/eastern-orthodoxy-gains-new-followers-in-america/.

Further Reading and Resources

Lippy, Charles H., and Peter W. Williams, eds. *Encyclopedia of Religion in America*. Washington, DC: CQ Press, 2010, "Eastern Orthodox Tradition and Heritage" (II, 577–584) and "Eastern Orthodoxy" (II, 585–591).

"How Orthodox Worship." https://www.youtube.com/watch?v=b6kOlaEXNGY

"Visiting an Orthodox Church." https://www.youtube.com/watch?v=aLuFlrHdUpQ

19

Christianity: Pentecostal and Holiness

> The 1967 documentary Holy Ghost People is a live recording of a Pentecostal service in a small Appalachian town where participants speak in tongues, give testimonies and, at the end, handle rattlesnakes. The point of this extreme behavior is to give witness in their belief in literally imitating the injunction in Mark 16:17–18.
>
> *They shall take up serpents; and if they drink any deadly thing, it shall not hurt them; they shall lay hands on the sick, and they shall recover.*
>
> The use of live snakes for worship is prohibited by law in most states, but continues to flourish in some remote parts of Appalachia. It should not be mistaken as standard Pentecostal practice, but it does represent the extremes to which biblical literalism can be taken.

Introduction

Membership Statistics.

Precise figures for Pentecostalism – a movement rather than a single denomination – are hard to come by, especially for Black churches. Total numbers for the United States are certainly in the tens of millions. The movement is the fastest growing in the world, with special success in Africa and Latin America and among American Hispanics. Early 2020s statistics for some of the larger denominations are:[1]

Assemblies of God:	3,233,385
Church of God (Cleveland TN):	1,074,047
COGIC (Churches of God in Christ, predominantly African American):	3,800,000
Foursquare Church:	350,000

The situation with Holiness churches is similar. The following are numbers for some of the largest denominations:

Church of the Nazarene:	2,640,216 (2020)[2]
Church of God (Anderson IN):	225,753 (2020)[3]

Historical Overview

During the late nineteenth century, a number of Methodists broke off from the parent denomination on the grounds that the latter had become too comfortable with middle-class values and lifestyles. This protest took form under the name Holiness, an Evangelical movement that rejected not only Methodism but a whole array of cultural practices that included smoking, drinking, movies, bobbed hair, and neckties, all of which they believed to be "worldly." Central to Holiness has been John Wesley's doctrine of "Entire Sanctification," the idea that not only is the Christian capable of justification – salvation – but also "Entire Sanctification," the freedom from voluntary sinfulness. Denominations coalesced within the movement, including the Church of God (Anderson, IN) and the Church of the Nazarene.

Pentecostalism is rooted in Holiness beliefs and practices, and by 1900 had begun to take on an identity of its own. In addition to Holiness emphases, Pentecostals believe that gifts of the Holy Spirit received by the earliest Christians – speaking in tongues, faith healing, prophesying – are accessible today through proper worship, prayer, and belief. With newly acquired middle-class status, Pentecostals have also entered the Evangelical middle-class mainstream.

Some larger (majority White) Pentecostal denominations include the Church of God (Cleveland, Tennessee) and the Missouri-based Assemblies of God.

Both Holiness and Pentecostal groups have Black and White counterparts, and are regionally concentrated in the South – although, like Evangelicalism in general, they have become more of a national phenomenon in recent decades. Congregations may range in size from small, rented storefronts to megachurches, although their status a century ago as "churches of the disinherited" is by no means universally accurate today. Many today are politically conservative, especially on social issues such as abortion. Hispanics, especially Mexicans, have joined in considerable numbers in recent years along with other Evangelical churches.

Scripture and Holidays

Pentecostals share many orientations and practices, such as an intense focus on scripture, with other Evangelicals. Worship shares features with other Evangelicals, especially in megachurches with praise bands and songs. The most distinctive feature of worship is the use of testimonials – personal accounts of the experience of salvation and the receipt of the Holy Spirit – and the practice of speaking in tongues – glossolalia – that consists of a free flow of syllables supposedly Spirit-inspired. Faith healing, prophesying, and exercises such as the "Jericho march" in imitation of Joshua and his followers are other Pentecostal practices that distinguish them from other Evangelical churches. "Praise music" is now standard for many Holiness and Pentecostal churches, while an older Gospel tradition still survives and in the past strongly influenced pop stars such as Jerry Lee Lewis and Elvis Presley.

Common Misunderstandings, Stereotypes, and Classroom Concerns

Practices such as speaking in tongues may seem alien to non-Pentecostals and require some explanation, preferably from students of Pentecostal background. The exotic practice of handling snakes is probably unfamiliar to most students, especially outside Appalachia, and may also need explanation.

Culturally Responsive Pedagogy

Are there Holiness and/or Pentecostal churches in your area? If so, where are they located? Does their location give you any hints as to how they relate to the broader society?

Notes

1 Source: https://en.wikipedia.org/wiki/List_of_Pentecostal_denominations.
2 Source: https://en.wikipedia.org/wiki/Church_of_the_Nazarene.
3 Source: https://en.wikipedia.org/wiki/Church_of_God_(Anderson,_Indiana).

Further Reading and Resources

"Don Rich: A Moment of Time" (Holiness Preaching). https://www.youtube.com/watch?v=cF3Nek6VFsk&list=PLkxPru8vZTJ7X8yCTc9b7YiVVC7UWTkFm
"Holy Ghost Dismissal" (Black Pentecostalism). https://www.youtube.com/watch?v=NVYEMx3PInE
"Holy Ghost People" (Snake Handling Documentary). https://www.youtube.com/watch?v=QZla4kutklM
Lippy, Charles H., and Peter W. Williams, eds. *Encyclopedia of Religion in America*. Washington, DC: CQ Press, 2010, "Holiness Denominational Family" (II, 1013–1020) and "Holiness Movement" (II, 1021–1026).
"There Is Power in the Blood" (Pentecostal Gospel Music). https://www.youtube.com/watch?v=kj4qNrCcato&list=PLAAZx_DduUXL2lzUXFr1yo8GU_Q-ijYJD
"What Are Pentecostal and Charismatic Churches?" https://www.youtube.com/watch?v=jXekCv1EKrE

20

Christianity: Presbyterian and Other Reformed Churches

If you picture a traditional white wooden church on a village green, the odds are good that it is a church in a Reformed denomination. The Reformed churches, most prominently the Presbyterians and the Congregationalists, are some of the oldest churches in the country. They established congregations in cities and small towns across the nation. They saw themselves as a key part of the Protestant establishment – attracting the leaders of society and setting the tone of the culture. Eight U.S. presidents were members of a Reformed church (second only to the Episcopal Church with 11). Membership in these denominations has declined in recent decades, but they still have an influence beyond their numbers.

Introduction

Membership statistics

Presbyterian Church USA: 1,140,665[1]
Presbyterian Church in America: 393,528 (2023)[2]
United Church of Christ (Congregational): 712,296 (2022)[3]
(Dutch) Reformed Church in America: 84,957 (2023)[4]
Christian Reformed Church: 189,753 (2024) (includes United States and Canada)[5]

Historical Overview

The Reformed tradition is a collection of Christian denominations with roots in Switzerland, England, and Scotland. It is made up of many denominations, the best known of which are Presbyterian or Congregationalist. They are known for their commitment to the Bible, their relatively simple worship services, and their social engagement.

This tradition is part of the larger Protestant Reformation of sixteenth-century Europe. Its most influential figure was John Calvin, a French lawyer, minister, and theologian. He was particularly active in the Swiss city of Geneva. Like Martin Luther, Calvin challenged the practices of the Roman Catholic Church. He based his theology on his interpretation of the Bible. He worked to purify the church's worship services and opposed the idea of earning salvation through deeds or donations. In its place Calvin emphasized God's absolute sovereignty, which included God's preordaining the entirety of humankind, some for eternal salvation, and some for damnation, a doctrine called predestination. The concept was central to Calvin's thought, but is rarely embraced in Reformed churches today.

Calvin's ideas, especially his focus on purifying church practice, spread from Switzerland across Europe. Soon there were large Reformed churches in the Netherlands, Germany, France, and Hungary. They followed Calvin's theology and held relatively simple worship services in their own languages. Some members of those churches migrated to North America and brought their Reformed faith with them, often speaking their home language. The Reformed Church in America and the Christian Reformed Church, for instance, were founded by Dutch migrants; those churches still have many members of Dutch descent.

Some of the most prominent Reformed denominations in the United States today trace their history back to churches established in the British Isles. The biggest distinction between them is their *polity*, or church governance. Many of the Calvinists in Scotland believed that their churches should be governed by elders – ministers and laymen chosen by members of the congregation. A local church would choose its own elders, who would choose leaders for all the churches in their region, who would choose leaders for all the churches in the country. This polity became known as Presbyterian, from the Greek word presbyteros, for "elder." Many of the Calvinists in England, however, believed that each congregation should govern itself, with no other organization telling them what to believe or do. This polity became known as Congregationalist.

These English-speaking Calvinists came to North America as well. Some English Congregationalists who were particularly focused on purifying the church from non-biblical practices came to be known as Puritans. They settled in New England in the 1620s and 1630s, becoming particularly dominant in Massachusetts and Connecticut. These Congregationalists dominated New England's religious life until the early 1800s, when their hegemony in greater Boston was challenged by their more liberal counterparts, the Unitarians. Their congregational polity meant that local churches could determine their own theologies and practices. This led to some radical politics among the members. Many members embraced the abolition of slavery and were active in the Underground Railroad. The first woman minister in an American church was Antoinette Brown, ordained by a Congregational church in 1852. This openness also led the Congregationalists to merge with other churches. In 1931 they merged with the Christian Church; those denominations joined with two other Reformed churches, established by German-speaking immigrants, in 1957 to form the United Church of Christ. The UCC, as it is often called, is now well known for its theological liberalism and social activism, with a strong emphasis on inclusion. It was the first denomination to ordain an openly gay person in 1972.

The Presbyterians began to arrive in the American colonies in the eighteenth century, largely brought by immigrants from Scotland. It first took denominational form in 1789. They settled throughout the American colonies but were particularly dominant in the mid-Atlantic region. Its leaders established seminaries to train its ministers; the first independent seminary in the United States was Princeton Theological Seminary, founded in 1812. The seminary's graduates established congregations through

Virginia, the Carolinas, and west into Kentucky and Tennessee. They shared a common commitment to Calvin's theology and the centrality of the Bible, but the denomination divided into several factions over issues of theology and, ultimately, slavery, much like the Methodists. Subsequent splits occurred early in the twentieth century over the fundamentalism controversy, and later over, like Methodists and others, issues of gender and sexuality. The Orthodox Presbyterian Church was established in 1936 and the Presbyterian Church in America in 1973. Sometimes however, Presbyterians have merged as well as divided. The Presbyterians' North-South schism over slavery was overcome in 1983, when the two regional denominations reunited to form The Presbyterian Church in the United States, the largest Presbyterian denomination in America. Ongoing controversies over social issues have led, however, to continuing division within the Presbyterian movement.

While once the social and economic peers of Episcopalians, both the United Church of Christ and the Presbyterian Church in the United States have seen strikingly diminished membership and influence beginning in the later twentieth century in the face of competition from Evangelicals on one side and "nones" – the religiously unaffiliated – from the other.

Scripture and Holidays

Presbyterian worship is squarely in the Reformed tradition, with an emphasis on Scripture reading and preaching. It shares Bible translations with other "mainline" denominations as well as the common lectionary. Other, perhaps, than Reformation Day (which coincides with Halloween), its holidays are the same as other mainline groups. Presbyterian hymnals similarly draw on a common body of hymns from the Reformation till the present.

Common Misunderstandings

Presbyterians are squarely in the "mainline" family of American denominations. Their practices and lifestyle do not differ in any observable way from other middle-class Americans.

Culturally Responsive Pedagogy

A fundamental question underlying the founding of the Reformed denominations was about the structure and purpose of the church. That is why some of them have named themselves for how they are governed – presbyterian or congregational. To understand these denominations, you might talk about those questions. What is the purpose of the church? What is the right structure for the church? Who should have power? Who should be included or excluded? Who draws those boundaries?

Notes

1 Source: https://pcusa.org/news-storytelling/news/2023/5/1/pcusa-church-membership-still-decline.
2 Source: https://pcanet.org/.
3 https://www.ucc.org/wp-content/uploads/2024/03/2023statisticalreport.v11webUPDATED.pdf.
4 Source: https://en.wikipedia.org/wiki/Reformed_Church_in_America.
5 Source: https://www.crcna.org/yearbook.

Further Reading and Resources

"An Outsider Visits a Presbyterian Church." https://www.youtube.com/watch?v=tVX0D5WbXsw

Balmer, Randall H., and John Fitzmier. *The Presbyterians*. Westport, CT: Greenwood, 1994.

Lippy, Charles H., and Peter W. Williams, eds. *Encyclopedia of Religion in America*. Washington, DC: CQ Press, 2010, "Congregationalists" (I, 488–); "Dutch Reformed" (I, 569–); ("Presbyterians: Colonial" (III, 1753–1758); "Presbyterians: Nineteenth Century" (III, 1759–1767); "Presbyterians: Since the Nineteenth Century" (1768–); "Reformed Denominational Family" (IV, 1838–).

Post, Margaret Rowland, and Thomas Dipko. *History and Program of the United Church of Christ*. Cleveland, OH: United Church Press, 2007.

"United Church of Christ History and Polity." https://www.youtube.com/watch?v=_m2HesJAoQ8

21

Christianity: Quakers (Friends)

> The smiling gentleman on the box of Quaker Oats, which you have perhaps enjoyed at breakfast, traces back to the company's founding in 1877. Although Quakers (more officially known as "Friends") no longer wear the eighteenth-century garb displayed on the oatmeal logo by "Larry" – as contemporary Friends have dubbed him – this garb, simple by the standards of its day, was chosen by the company's followers as projecting good quality and honest value, in line with the movements for dietary reform promoted during the same era with the invention of the corn flake and other cold cereals.

Introduction

Population Statistics (2022) for the United States: about 80,000 for all branches.[1]

Historical Overview

The Quakers – or, more formally, the *Society of Friends* – originated in seventeenth century England among the followers of George Fox. Fox, a prophetic figure, denounced traditional Christianity as stifling the Inner Light – analogous to the Holy Spirit – that

DOI: 10.4324/9781003405894-21

dwelled in all and made all people worthy of equal social status and respect. The movement rejected military service and formal worship, preferring a gathering of believers without a formal ministry who met in silence until someone was prompted to speak by this Inner Light.

Fox's movement was brought to the New World by William Penn, who in 1682 established Philadelphia as the "city of brotherly love" where the Friends could live in harmony and practice their distinctive form of worship in freedom. Quakers there became prosperous through their staunch work ethic, reputation for honesty, and rejection of "worldliness." Their pacifism, however, became problematic as demands for support of late colonial warfare led to compromises and eventually complete withdrawal from the government.

During the early nineteenth century, a series of splits over a variety of issues led to the formation of several different branches of the tradition. Probably best-known today is the Philadelphia Annual Meeting, embraced mainly by socially conscious, well-educated Quakers. Their focus is on peace-making, both through their opposition to war as well as positive efforts to eliminate the causes of suffering and violence. Like Unitarian Universalists, such Quakers are likely to be found in communities with high educational levels. Other Quakers, some traditional and others Evangelical, can be found in historic centers such as Richmond, Indiana, and the North Carolina Piedmont region.

Scripture and Holidays

Quakers use the Bible much as do other Christians, with no preferred translations and no official interpretation. Worship takes place at weekly meetings, which may be "programmed" or "unprogrammed." Unprogrammed worship – "silent meetings" – is quiet, which is broken only when someone is stirred to do so by the "Inner Light," the aspect of the Divine found within each believer. Meetings are held on the "First Day" – Sunday – and holidays such as Christmas and Easter are not observed on the premise that time and place cannot be holy.

Common Misunderstandings, Stereotypes, and Classroom Concerns

Many students may carry with them the image of "Larry" as a typical Quaker. Although it is hard to generalize about a tradition that has so many and differing branches, many if not most Quakers today do not differ visibly from most other Americans. The use of "thee" and "thou" instead of you – a practice that originated in the seventeenth century when English, like many other languages spoken today, still distinguished between everyday address (thou/thee) and formal, deferential address (you) – was intended as a protest against social class distinctions reflected in this usage. Most Quakers today have abandoned such distinctions, but sometimes make a point of refusing to respect social rank. In times of military draft, Quakers have helped establish a legal exemption from active service involving violence – "conscientious objection" – but are generally willing to participate in alternative service such as medical work.

Culturally Responsive Pedagogy

Have a screening of the classic film "High Noon," in which the sheriff's Quaker wife faces a stark decision between defending her husband and her faith's pacifist teachings. Discuss the ethical dilemmas involved in belonging to a sect with beliefs judged radical by the dominant society.

Note

1 Friends World Committee for Consultation, https://fwcc.world/learn/quaker-tradition-practice/.

Further Reading and Resources

Lippy, Charles H., and Peter W. Williams, eds. *Encyclopedia of Religion in America*. Washington, DC: CQ Press, 2010.
"Quakers: Through the Nineteenth Century" IV, 1807–1814.
"Quakers: Since the Nineteenth Century," 1815–1820.

22

Christianity: Restorationist (Churches of Christ, Disciples of Christ)

> It was said of Alexander Campbell – founder of the Restorationist Movement – that he never claimed to be infallible, but was never known to have been wrong.

Introduction

U.S. Membership:

Disciples of Christ: 277,864 (2022)[1]
Churches of Christ: 1,087,599 (2022)[2]

Historical Overview

The Disciples of Christ is the smallest of the Mainline denominations, and arose in the early nineteenth century on the Ohio and Kentucky frontiers through Presbyterians preaching a basic theology which taught that "where the Scriptures speak; we speak; where the Scriptures are silent, we are silent." The early Disciples rejected denominations and creeds, and maintained that the plain words of the Bible were a sufficient guide to Christian belief and practice. Like the Baptists, they rejected the baptism of infants as having no scriptural precedent. A disagreement between more liberal (urban) and conservative (rural) factions over the use of non-scriptural musical instruments – organs and pianos – in worship resulted in a split between the Disciples and a more Fundamentalist aggregation of conservative churches calling themselves Churches of Christ.

The Disciples and their more conservative counterparts have been most numerous in the areas where they originated – Kentucky and southern Ohio – as well as in contiguous Southern states and those of the Old Southwest – Tennessee, Arkansas, Texas, and Oklahoma. Like American Baptists, Disciples are ecumenically inclined and open to local mergers or other cooperative arrangements with like-minded denominations.

Scripture and Holidays

Restoration Movement churches celebrate the Lord's Supper weekly, and practice "adult" believer's baptism by immersion. Clergy are not generally required to bless the elements or say the words of institution. These roles are generally carried out by lay elders, with deacons serving. These liturgical activities are not considered sacraments, but sacramental. For Disciples of Christ, the table – not altar – is central, and all are invited to participate regardless of their denominational background and often, any other status: marital, ethnicity, gender, gender orientation, etc. Because each local church is autonomous, it is up to each congregation whether they will be welcoming and affirming of LGBT+ people.

The "independent" Christian and Churches of Christ, are more Evangelical. They celebrate the Lord's Supper weekly. Their hymnody is more likely to be praise music, which has largely replaced the earlier "revival and gospel" music.

The non-instrumental Churches of Christ are bibliocentric, and generally believe that the Bible is the inerrant and infallible Word of God. Churches of Christ practice believer's baptism by immersion and celebrate the Lord's Supper. Clergy – always men – are not necessarily seminary trained.

Common Misunderstandings, Stereotypes, and Classroom Concerns

Outside a band stretching southwest from Ohio, Restorationist denominations are not well known. Disciples are the smallest of the mainline denominations, which Churches of Christ fall within the Evangelical/Fundamentalist spectrum. Other than some of the distinctive practices, such as the powers of the laity and, for Churches of Christ, a refusal to use instrumental music (on the grounds that it is not explicitly mentioned in Christian scripture), there is little in this tradition that schools would need to be aware of.

Notes

1 Walton, Jeffrey, "Analysis: Disciples of Christ Suffer Massive Membership Drop Post-2019," *The Roys Report*. September 15, 2023.
2 Royster, Carl H., "Churches of Christ in the United States," *21st Century Christian*. June 2020.

Further Reading and Resources

"Church Splits: Churches of Christ and Christian Churches (Disciples of Christ)." https://www.youtube.com/watch?v=Qx5O2CjYQAc

Lippy, Charles H., and Peter W. Williams, eds. *Encyclopedia of Religion in America*. Washington, DC: CQ Press, 2010, "Churches of Christ" (I, 460–4650); "Disciples of Christ" (I, 558–563); "Stone-Campbell Movement" (IV, 2161–2165).

23

Christianity: Roman and Eastern Catholic

> Prior to the Vatican II Ecumenical Council of the early 1960s, American Protestants and others sometimes referred to Roman Catholics as "mackerel snappers," humorously or sometimes with malice. This nickname came from the Catholic practice of abstaining from meat on Fridays or other designated days as a penitential practice in memory of the day of Jesus's crucifixion. Although eating fish ("mackerel") specifically was never mandated, the practice was widely adopted as part of American Catholic culture. The nickname rapidly faded after Vatican II, which reduced the no-meat requirement to Ash Wednesday, Good Fridays, and the Fridays of Lent. This and other changes in letter and spirit ended many practices that had previously distinguished Catholics from other Christians and had constituted a boundary that separated the religious camps.

Membership

Approximately 52,000,000 (adults) (2023)[1]

DOI: 10.4324/9781003405894-23

Historical Overview

The term "catholic" derives from a Greek word meaning "universal," and in early Christian centuries was embraced by most followers of the new religion who accepted Paul's teaching that "in Christ there is neither Jew nor Greek" (Galatians 3:28). The Nicene Creed, adopted by the worldwide (*ecumenical*) council of bishops convened by the Emperor Constantine in 325 CE to standardize belief across the empire, contained the phrase "We believe in one, holy, catholic, and apostolic church," whether those professing the creed were from the Eastern (Greek-speaking) or Western (Latin-speaking) portions of that empire. As Western Christianity began to coalesce in the West around the authority of the Bishop of Rome (the Pope), the East remained decentralized in organization, recognizing the historic centers of early Christianity, and rejecting claims to supremacy developing around the Pope in Rome. The centrality of Papal authority in the West would not be seriously challenged until the Protestant Reformation of the early sixteenth century, and still remains an obstacle to any formal Christian organizational unity.

The expression of Christianity that developed in the medieval West – loosely defined as areas in which Latin remained the dominant language for religious worship, scholarly discourse, and governmental business – flourished as the old Empire that vanished with the fall of Rome to barbarian invaders in 395 opened the path for Church dominance. The coronation of Charlemagne as Holy Roman Emperor by Pope Leo III in 800 ushered in an era of several centuries – the "Middle Ages" – in which popes and emperors both collaborated and squabbled over secular power, but during which no plausible challenges to the religious supremacy of the Bishop of Rome emerged. Although the on-the-ground pluralistic reality of medieval Christianity was messier than depicted in more romanticized later interpretations, the Church did unify and channel religious sentiment into a force that shaped the great Gothic cathedrals and the literary work of Chaucer and Dante.

The Protestant Reformation that reached full power in the earlier 1500s fed on religious, political, and social discontent that had been building up for some time. It put a permanent end to the notion that Europe was co-equivalent with a putative "Christendom" in which Church and State presided more or less harmoniously in a society established for God's glory. Britain, the Netherlands, and considerable portions of Germany, Switzerland, and Hungary rejected papal authority, while new expressions of "Protestant" Christianity survived and flourished under the aegis of emergent centralized national governments such as the Tudor dynasty in England. By the 1870s, the unification of Germany and Italy into consolidated nation-states further eroded the political power of the Church as, most dramatically, the Papal States, hitherto an independent nation under direct papal control, were absorbed into a newly unified secular Italian government. The ensuing attitude of belligerence and beleaguerment by the Pope, who saw himself as "the prisoner of the Vatican," resulted in an alienation of papal leadership from modern society and thought during the same period in which Catholicism in the United States was rapidly expanding and consolidating.

This same sense of beleaguerment expressed itself as well among American Catholics, who by the turn of the twentieth century had grown into a vast community within the American religious landscape. Prior to the Civil War, Irish Catholics fleeing the potato famine that was destroying their English-ruled nation arrived in the great cities of the East Coast, such as Boston, New York, and Philadelphia. The myriad of smaller states that would become Germany in 1870 were divided religiously, but many Catholics fled with their Protestant and Jewish countryfolk to seek prosperity and liberty in the area of settlement known as the "German Triangle" bounded loosely by Cincinnati, Milwaukee, and St. Louis. Following the Civil War, an even larger influx of Catholic newcomers fled economic and political catastrophes in Central Europe, including Lithuanians, Poles, Slovaks, Hungarians, Croatians, and Italians. Many of these, with their Eastern Orthodox counterparts, found opportunity in the emergent industrial cities of the Great Lakes, where unskilled labor was in seemingly endless demand, even at great risk to those thus employed in Chicago's stockyards, Detroit's auto factories, and Pittsburgh's steel mills.

By now the Irish had come to dominate America's Catholic community, and their clergy and bishops sought simultaneously to provide facilities for worship and a cradle-to-grave infrastructure of educational and social institutions. The Catholic leadership went to great lengths not only to provide spiritual and material care for their charges but also institutional and ideological protection from Protestant-dominated schools and other cultural challenges. Just as the Pope in Rome retreated into a posture of belligerent self-defense from the twin threats of Protestantism and secularism, so did American Catholic leadership work to establish a social and cultural "ghetto" that would simultaneously permit Catholic immigrants and their children to enjoy the benefits of American economic and political opportunity while avoiding the threats and temptations of a broader society that perceived the Catholic Church as inimical to American democratic institutions.

Following World War I, which put an end for many decades to large-scale immigration from Catholic Europe, a distinctively American Catholic subculture began to make its mark on the broader society. Some of its more visible features included:

1. Bishops, priests, and nuns (sisters) who made their presence known through distinctive garb, especially the elaborate habits favored by some female religious orders.
2. Cathedrals and cathedral-sized parish churches that towered above surrounding ethnic Catholic neighborhoods.
3. An educational system of parochial elementary schools stretching across the nation, later augmented by diocesan high schools, colleges, and universities staffed by both male and female religious orders; seminaries to train and socialize aspiring priests; monasteries and convents; and hospitals, orphanages, old-age facilities, and cemeteries, all designed to serve and to insulate.
4. A defensive and often antagonistic relationship with Protestant and secular institutions whom Catholics viewed, often with good reason, as hostile both to

Catholic immigrants and their religious institutions and cultures. Mixed marriages were deeply suspect, as was the attendance of Catholic youth at non-Catholic schools.
5. A close association with working-class culture, labor unions, and the Democratic Party.
6. Success in urban politics in cities such as Boston and Chicago with substantial Catholic populations, but also a "glass ceiling" preventing Catholic access to the highest reaches of government.

This "ghetto" era began to end with the emergence of a critically minded Catholic intelligentsia in the 1950s; a flow of Catholic veterans into the middle classes and religiously blended suburbs courtesy of the GI Bill; the election of an Irish-American Catholic, John F. Kennedy, to the American presidency in 1960 in the face of organized Protestant opposition; and the convening of the Vatican II Ecumenical Council by Pope (Saint) John XXIII in 1961. The latter gathering had as its agenda the modernization of the Catholic Church through a reform of the liturgy, the ending of suspicion of and segregation from the secular world, cooperation with Protestant and other religious traditions, and a diminishing emphasis on the distinction between clergy and laity.

Post-Vatican II American Catholicism initiated a rapid if sometimes grudging end to the perception of American Catholics as "other'; instead, they were now simply Americans with some distinctive beliefs and practices that differentiated them from other Christians who no longer perceived one another as enemies. Some manifestations of this new openness to the broader society and other religions were:

1. A de-emphasis on the need for young Catholics to attend religiously oriented schools, resulting in an influx of Catholics into public schools and the repurposing of older inner-city schools toward the education of minorities.
2. The entry of many Catholic-affiliated colleges and universities into a broader world of academic discourse.

3. A rapid dropping-off in numbers of clergy and women in religious orders, as nuns were no longer needed or available to staff Catholic schools in great numbers, and as the attractions of secular vocations steered young Catholic men and women into other, non-celibate professions. As the number of priests grew lower than that needed to maintain parish life, foreign-born clergy from third-world areas such as Africa and the Philippines were imported to fill the gap.

Since the 1960s, most American Catholics of European ancestry have attained solidly middle-class or even higher social status. Ethnic loyalties have become more sentimental than functional, and intermarriage among Catholic groups as well with those of other religions has largely ended the combination of religious, ethnic, and class identity that had characterized their forebears. Divorce, though technically forbidden – Church-sanctioned annulments provide a functional alternative for those who care to stay within the boundaries of Church teaching – makes Catholics closer to the broader American populace in social mores. Abortion remains a "wedge issue," especially among bishops, but laypeople are equally divided among political parties and social views, and such traditional issues have been taken up by many Evangelicals as well.

The largest cultural divisions within the American Catholic community are no longer between Irish and, say, Germans, but rather between English- and Spanish-speakers. Even the latter are far from homogeneous: Puerto Ricans in New York City, Cubans in Miami, and Mexicans in Los Angeles share a language and religion but often have very different religious cultures. Distinctive practices of Mexican American Catholicism, for instance, include devotion to the Virgin of Guadalupe, a central symbol of Mexican identity, and the *quinceañera*, a coming-of-age ceremony for teenage girls with religious dimensions. On the other hand, considerable numbers of Latino/as have been attracted to Pentecostal and other Evangelical congregations which are emotionally expressive – for example, speaking in tongues; Spanish-speaking; and more attuned with Hispanic cultural practices than most large, English-speaking Catholic parishes. It is these Catholics who present the largest challenge for American schools, but more because of linguistic and other cultural challenges than anything specifically religious. Catholic schools themselves, many now serving inner-city clienteles, are at least equally confronted by these dilemmas as are the public schools.

Another variety of Catholics is a group of churches known as Uniate or Eastern (Byzantine Rite) Catholic. These churches, with origins mainly in southeastern Europe and the Middle East, were originally aligned with Eastern Orthodoxy, but split with the latter to come under Roman Catholic jurisdiction. Unlike traditional Roman Catholics, and like the Orthodox, they allow married clergy and follow Byzantine (Orthodox) liturgies. They are mainly found in Great Lakes states where their predecessors settled to work in mining and industry in the late nineteenth century.

Scripture and Holidays

Roman Catholic worship is similar to that of other liturgical traditions such as Anglicanism, Eastern Orthodoxy, and Lutheranism. It is sacramental, focused on seven rituals understood to be channels of divine grace – baptism, the Eucharist, reconciliation (penance), confirmation, matrimony, priestly ordination, and anointing of the sick/dying. The Eucharist (Holy Communion) is celebrated weekly on Sundays or Saturday evenings, and commemorates the Last Supper through the administration of bread and wine to recipients. Catholics follow a standard Christian liturgical calendar, with the addition of certain holy days honoring the Virgin Mary. (Devotion to Mary has historically been a source of division between Catholics and Protestants, although it is also observed by Eastern Orthodox and Anglo-Catholics.)

Common Misunderstandings, Stereotypes, and Classroom Concerns

In regions where Catholics are scarce, especially the rural South, some may find Catholic rituals somewhat mysterious in its complexity. Now that the United States has had two Catholic presidents (Kennedy and Biden), earlier fears about Catholic governmental figures being subject to Vatican control have largely faded, although lingering anti-Catholic sentiments and mythology may need to be defused.

Since Vatican II, social and cultural differences between Catholics and other religious groups have diminished considerably. On Ash Wednesday, Catholic students may come to school with a cross of ashes on their foreheads, a symbol of mortality also observed by some other Christians. This could be a target for "othering" such students, which may call for an intervention and explanation. Accommodations should be made for abstinence from meat on Fridays during Lent. Most Catholic churches offer sufficient alternatives for worship outside school hours when a holy day falls on a weekday so that further accommodation should not usually be necessary.

The multiethnic makeup of the American Catholic community, especially of Mexicans and other Spanish-speakers, involves a combination of religious and cultural practices. Such groups practice a common Catholicism which may utilize Spanish or other languages during services and festivals. The quinceañera is a rite of passage for girls on their fifteenth birthdays, which combines a religious service with an elaborate party. This and other customs, such as mariachi Masses and the veneration of the Virgin of Guadalupe, should provide no problems during school time, but might need to be explained to "Anglos" if their community does not have a significant Spanish-speaking presence.

Culturally Responsive Pedagogy

In an area where there are multiple Catholic churches, discussing the reasons for their multiplicity could be an avenue into understanding the "catholicity" of the Catholic Church. Similarly, the division within the Catholic community over abortion and women's ordination might be worth a carefully managed discussion.

Note

1   Justin Nortey, Patricia Tevington, and Gregory A. Smith, "9 Facts about U.S. Catholics." April 12, 2024, https://www.pewresearch.org/short-reads/2024/04/12/9-facts-about-us-catholics/.

Further Reading and Resources

"A Protestant Tours an Amazing Byzantine Church." https://www.youtube.com/watch?v=ii0jJecSIFw

"A Protestant Tours a Catholic Cathedral." https://www.youtube.com/watch?v=yOlU_4pzft4

Brehm, Stephanie N. *America's Most Famous Catholic (According to Himself: Stephen Colbert and American Religion in the Twenty-First Century*. New York: Fordham University Press, 2019.

Lippy, Charles H., and Peter W. Williams, eds. *Encyclopedia of Religion in America*. Washington, DC: CQ Press, 2010, "Roman Catholicism: African American Catholics," IV, 1954–1959; "RC: Catholics in the Atlantic Colonies," IV, 1960–1962; "RC, Catholics in the New Nation and the Early Republic," IV, 1963–1967; "RC: The Impact of Immigration and the Nineteenth Century," IV, 1968–1975; "RC: The Age of the Catholic Ghetto," IV, 1976–1983; "RC: The Cold War and Vatican II," IV, 1984–1987; "RC: The Later Twentieth Century," IV, 1988–1992; "RC: Early Twenty-First-Century Issues," IV, 1993–1995; "RC: Cultural Impact," IV, 1996–2003; "RC: French Influence," IV, 2004–2007; "RC: Tradition and Heritage," IV, 2008–2018.

Orsi, Robert Anthony. *The Madonna of 115th Street: Faith and Community in Italian Harlem, 1880–1950*. New Haven, CT and London: Yale University Press, 1985.

"Why Is Our Lady of Guadalupe So Important to Mexico?" https://www.youtube.com/watch?v=JaMgGaRxhJ0

24

Christianity: Seventh-day Adventists

Although many religious traditions have used teachings about food and its uses as part of their symbolic systems, the Seventh-day Adventists are perhaps the only such tradition to have generated an entire industry based on food. During the middle of the nineteenth century, many Americans suffered from dyspepsia, a chronic intestinal ailment resulting from eating heavy, greasy foods. Seventh-day Adventism recognized the relationship between physical and spiritual health, and promoted a vegetarian diet as well as abstinence from stimulating beverages such as alcohol and coffee.

The brothers John Harvey and Will Keith Kellogg, who had settled in Battle Creek MI, were active Adventists who recognized and promoted the virtues of a light diet at Adventist headquarters in Battle Creek MI. The result was the corn flake, which Will Keith turned into an entire industry. Charles Post, who had also discovered the virtues of such a diet, invented an alternative to coffee in the form of Postum, as well as the ever-popular Grapenuts cereal, which contained neither grapes nor nuts.

Introduction

Membership statistics: 1,257,884 (USA and Canada) (2023)[1]

Historical Overview

Seventh-day Adventism is a religious tradition that originated in upstate New York in the 1840s. In the wake of the "Great Disappointment" of 1844, when the prophecies of William Miller about the imminent return – "advent" – of Jesus to earth had proven inaccurate, one of his disciples rallied to revive his movement with some new twists. Ellen G. White claimed to have received a number of revelations that built on but modified Miller's visions, and avoided the difficulties that ensue from making too specific a prediction about Jesus's second appearance on earth.

The movement was organized as a denomination, based in southern Michigan, in 1863. Adventist beliefs are mostly similar to those of Evangelicals, with some exceptions. Saturday rather than Sunday is observed as the Sabbath, and Adventists hold to the expectation that Jesus will return in the near future – *premillennialism*. Most distinctive is the SDA emphasis on health: they observe a vegetarian diet, refrain from the consumption of alcohol and tobacco, and maintain a network of hospitals in many parts of the United States and beyond that follow mainstream medical practices.

Scripture and Holidays

Adventist worship has one major difference from most Protestant practices: Saturday rather than Sunday is regarded as the Sabbath, a day reserved for worship. The Saturday Sabbath service begins with Sabbath School, followed by a gathering for a sermon, singing, and scripture reading. The Lord's Supper is observed quarterly, preceded by footwashing.

Common Misunderstandings, Stereotypes, and Classroom Concerns

Though Adventists, like Mormons, have some distinctive lifestyle practices, they for the most part present themselves as ordinary middle-class Americans. They maintain their own system of schools, but do not reject the broader society. Their presence in public schools does not present any particular issues, except for provisions for a meatless diet.

Culturally Responsive Pedagogy

If Adventism is the subject for classroom discussion, the relationship between physical and spiritual well-being might suggest itself as a topic.

Note

1   Ask an Adventist Friend, Seventh-day Adventist World Population and Demographics, https://www.askanadventistfriend.com/adventist-culture/seventh-day-adventist-world-population-and-demographics/.

Further Reading and Resources

Lippy, Charles H., and Peter W. Williams, eds. *Encyclopedia of Religion in America*. Washington, DC: CQ Press, 2010, "Adventism and Millennialism"(I, 12–20), "Adventist and Millennialist Denominational Families" (I, 21–24), "Seventh-day Adventists" (IV, 2065–2067).

"What Is the Seventh-day Adventist Church?" https://www.youtube.com/watch?v=p1fzHbSo9lM

25

Christianity: Unitarian Universalist

> During the nineteenth century, Unitarianism – later to merge with Universalism – was a prominent promoter of an optimistic view of God and humanity. A major spokesman, Harvard professor James Freeman Clarke, summarized its creed as "We believe in The Fatherhood of God, The Brotherhood of Man, The Leadership of Jesus, Salvation by Character, and The Progress of Mankind, onward and upward forever." Since the Unitarian movement originated in Boston and its influence remained centered there for some time, one wag paraphrased Clarke's beliefs as "the Fatherhood of God, the Brotherhood of Man, and the Neighborhood of Boston." However apt this might have seemed in Clarke's time, Unitarian Universalism today is spread throughout the United States and beyond but still professes the same concern for social reform and progress exemplified in Clarke's career and teachings.

Introduction

U.S. Membership: 152,958 (2024)[1]

History

Although Unitarians and Universalists both trace their earliest influences to Reformation-era Europe, they were established in America around the time of national independence, first in New England and then beyond – Unitarians in the Midwest and West, Universalists in the South. They shared a common rejection of Calvinism and, while Unitarians emphasized a positive appraisal of human character, Universalists stressed universal salvation. Regional and social class differences kept them institutionally separate until the two denominations united in 1961 to form the Unitarian Universalist Association (UUA).

UUs, as they are commonly known, differ in personal belief among themselves and actively promote theological inclusiveness. Some churches in the Boston area still regard themselves as liberal Christians, while others throughout the country are more inclined to think of themselves as humanists or seekers of truth. Congregations range from minister-led to lay-led. They are guided by the principles of Interdependence, Equity, Transformation, Pluralism, Generosity, and Justice, all focused on Love. They have for some time focused on social justice issues including the rights of women, minorities, LGBTQ and transgender persons, voting rights, systemic racism, and environmental justice. Sunday worship topics are quite diverse, and can range from consideration of contemporary or historic justice issues to appreciation of other religious traditions, the history of religion, and ethical or biblical discussions. The lighting of a chalice provides a ritual focus to worship or meditation. UUs tend to be well-educated and socially progressive.

Scriptures and Holidays

UUs respect the Hebrew and Christian scriptures and may utilize them in worship services, but also incorporate readings from other world religions and secular documents that deal with ethical and spiritual issues. They generally recognize Christian holidays such as Christmas and Easter, but may not observe them in a traditional fashion. Their hymnals include some traditionally Christian hymns edited to conform to UU beliefs and practices.

Common Misunderstandings

A frequent question about UUs is whether or not they are Christian or something other, such as "secular humanists." The answer varies from congregation to congregation and from individual to individual. Some older congregations in the Boston area define themselves as "liberal Christians," while others prefer terms such as "humanist." While their principles stress ethical issues, they avoid creeds and emphasize the right of individual choice and judgment. The First Unitarian Church of Dallas video cited below may prove helpful if these issues arise.

Note

1 Unitarian Universalist Association, Demographic and Statistical Information about Unitarian Universalism, https://www.uua.org/data/demographics/uua-statistics.

Further Reading and Resources

"Are Unitarian Universalists Christian?" (First Unitarian Church of Dallas). https://www.youtube.com/watch?v=nXTkUIxWuBg

Lippy, Charles H., and Peter W. Williams, eds. *Encyclopedia of Religion in America*. Washington, DC: CQ Press, 2010, "Unitarians" (2222–2227); "Unitarian Universalist Association" (2228–2030); "Universalists" (2231–2233).

UUA Website. https://www.uua.org/

Wikipedia on Unitarianism. https://en.wikipedia.org/wiki/Unitarian_Universalism

26

Hinduism: Overview

> In the ancient city of Varanasi (Benares), there are banyan trees that have thrived for centuries. Varanasi is one of the oldest continuously inhabited cities in the world. The banyan trees that thrive there tell a story of old and new intertwined together. Banyan trees have roots that grow out of their branches. These outer roots grow straight down to the ground, where they take root and mature into thick trunks. The descending roots of this remarkable tree often fuse with the bricks and stones of houses in Varanasi, creating an organic fusion of old and new. Like the fusion of ancient tree roots and newly made bricks, Hinduism has ancient roots that anchor new configurations. Chants that date back to 1500 BCE can be heard today on YouTube channels and in Bollywood musical sequences. WhatsApp groups convene for virtual worship. Hinduism, like the banyan tree, gives the impression of vast antiquity woven into ever-new arrangements.

Introduction

Considering Hinduism's growth and inventiveness, a person might wonder how the religion maintains its cohesion. One answer to the question is the power of ceremonial gestures and rituals to connect across vast stretches of time. Hinduism is often described as a performed religion. Many Hindus regard

FIGURE 26.1 A banyan tree with roots that grow down from the top

the correct performance of ceremonial gestures (orthopraxy) as the key mark of adherence. For those who place weight on how sacred actions are performed, the question of doctrinal correctness (orthodoxy) is less important. Hence innovations through time cohere and contribute to the stability of the religion if they are firmly anchored in ceremonial forms that are recognized as correct. Innovations take root and persist when they meet ceremonial standards. Orthopraxy also explains the unity within plurality that gives coherence to the vast pantheon of sacred beings that Hindus revere and the multiplicity of sacred texts that tell their stories. Hindus in India speak a variety of different languages and, in addition, have different sectarian affiliations. But when a Hindu from Varanasi meets a Hindu from Mumbai or Manchester, their linguistic and sectarian divides are easily overcome by a common language of ritual gestures. Ritual forms that draw on the sacred power of fire and water, sometimes combined (as when a lit lamp is placed on the surface of water), persist through the generations and give coherence and continuity to the endless inventiveness of Hinduism's banyan tree (Figure 26.1).

Before we explore the history of Hinduism, a word about language will be useful. One can read and listen to Hindu myths in Sanskrit, Hindi, Kannada, Malayalam, Tamil, and many other regional languages. Even major deities are often referred to by their regional names. When there are multiple versions of names of deities or scriptures, we have selected the Sanskrit forms rendered in English. Hence we have flattened some of the regional variations that make Hinduism a complex dish with many different flavors to savor.

Historical Overview

Hinduism is the third-largest religion in the world today, with over a billion adherents. India and Nepal have Hindu majority populations. While most Hindus live in Asian countries, there are Hindu communities all over the world. Many Hindus live today in the Middle East, in Africa, and in the Caribbean region. Hindu workers traveled to these and other places in the nineteenth century and made homes there. Due to this, you can visit a Hindu temple and see Hindu rituals in places as far apart as Kenya, on the east coast of Africa, and Trinidad, in the Caribbean. Twentieth- and twenty-first-century migration has brought Hindus to Europe, North America, and other places.

There are over 2.5 million Hindus in the United States today.[1] Many families who practice Hinduism in America today arrived after 1965, when national quotas on immigrants from Asia were removed. Hindus in America are some of the most successful migrants who have settled here. Indian Americans (a group that includes Hindus as well as adherents of Jainism, Sikhism, Islam, Christianity, Zoroastrianism, and other religions) have the highest education levels of any U.S. ethnic group. Indian Americans have made outstanding contributions to many forms of industry. For example, there is no group that excels Indian Americans when it comes to success in Information Technology.

The civilizations of the Indian subcontinent are among the oldest in the world, extending back to settlements along the Indus River that date to 3300 BCE. Another layer of civilization came with a group of nomadic, cattle-herding people from the Russian steppes. This group used the term Aryan ("noble") to refer to themselves. They spoke a language that is related to today's Sanskrit and worshipped with hymns collected in the four Vedas. Vedic chants and songs of offering form a foundational layer of Hinduism's sacred corpus, a source of mantras (sacred sounds) that Hindus intone today. Key themes in the Vedas indicate that there was ethnic mixing between those inside and those outside the Aryan fold. The caste system emerged from this mixing of the groups, enabling outsiders to join Vedic society, but relegating them to the lower stratum. Vedic society was hierarchical, with four main castes (divided into a multitude of subcastes) working together in interdependence to sustain a society conceived as an organic whole. At the top stood Brahmins, who built fire altars, communicated with deities in metered verse, memorized and orally transmitted those sacred verses to their descendants, and thus preserved what Hindus consider timeless wisdom that was originally heard by ancient sages and preserved in the four Vedic collections (the *Rig Veda*, the *Yajur Veda*, the *Sama Veda*, and the *Atharva Veda*). The next caste in the Vedic hierarchy is the warrior caste, including kings and less consequential rulers. In pre-modern times, this caste was charged with keeping the world free of human and demonic disruptions. Their religiously justified warfare and kingship supported righteous living according to dharma, the order of the universe that is the basis for moral action and the laws of nature. The next group in the hierarchy is the commoner caste: this group would have included a wide range of occupations, from agriculture to the work of merchants and artisans, all laboring to support the righteous order of the world. The lowest caste is the servant caste. The job of the servant caste was carrying off waste. Removing corpses, human and animal, and rendering animal corpses into food, clothing, and footwear was central to the sacred job description that gave members of this caste a livelihood that required little in the way of education. Finally, there were those groups that fell outside the caste system altogether, called "untouchables" by British administrators in colonial India. Today these groups prefer the name Dalit ("broken") or Bahujan ("the majority," "the masses").

The caste system has been the object of internal critique by Hindus since pre-modern times. Those who favor the devotional path often depict hierarchy as an obstacle that prevents an intimate relationship with God. The Indian Constitution bans discrimination on the basis of caste and the government has taken measures to reverse the effects of caste on Indian society.

Vedic religion centered on fire. A central ritual was the building of fire altars. Animals, milk, and other substances were offered, with the god of fire conveying these offerings to celestial deities. Immortality was not a goal of Vedic worship. Proper sacrificial activity was thought to bring monsoon rains at the appropriate time. Crops would flourish, herds would grow large, and humans, while mortal, would live long lives. The promise of immortality first appeared in the Upanishads, a series of sacred texts framed as secret dialogues between gurus and their students who sought the inner meaning of the commentaries on the Veda. Major Upanishads appear as early as the sixth century BCE, with minor Upanishads composed later. The Upanishads are considered to be mystical reflections on the Vedas. In the Vedas, the fire god Agni embodies the radiance of the sun, lightning, and all things that glow with heat. In ritual terms, Agni is the fiery mouth of the deities, a crucial way for humans to communicate with the distant deities. In the Upanishads, Agni appears as the inner principle of radiance that every human carries within. Building on old Vedic models of worship, the sages of the Upanishads suggest that one can perform a sacrifice without building a fire altar. One can simply offer food to the "universal Agni" that is the digestive fire in the stomach that metabolizes food. The universal presence of a deity like Agni, who is both within humans and outside us in the celestial sphere, was a template for the Upanishadic teachers who taught the idea that the divine is within a human being as well as outside.

By identifying with this inner divinity, the sages of the Upanishads offered an answer to students who were troubled by a new idea circulating in the Upanishadic era: the idea of reincarnation as an endless cycle of births and deaths. Upanishadic sages taught that realizing one's divine, immortal essence would ensure escape from the misery that comes with an unending cycle of birth, aging, sickness, death, and rebirth, especially rebirth in lower realms of existence such as animals or hells. Later philosophers, in a tradition called Vedanta (the wisdom that is the essence of the Vedas), systematized the teaching of the Upanishads. One school of Vedanta describes the unity of the One and Many, with a single Supreme Being manifest in many individual souls, like an ocean showing itself in individual waves. Another school of Vedanta taught that the Supreme Being is both the same as and inexplicably distinct from individual souls, with the difference between the two allowing for a relationship of love and devotion. Those who favor the devotional path express the love that binds the divine and the human by tending to icons of the divine at home or in the temple, singing hymns, reciting poetry, and performing dances and plays.

During the last few centuries BCE and the first few centuries CE, books of religious law (such as *The Laws of Manu*) were composed along with early versions of the *Mahabharata* and the *Ramayana*, beloved epics that tell the story of warriors. One section of the *Mahabharata* is the *Bhagavad Gita*, the "Song of the Lord," that recounts how the god Krishna taught the warrior Arjuna how to overcome a crisis on the battlefield by the practice of acting in the world without any attachment to the results of that action. Krishna revealed himself to Arjuna as the Supreme Being and offered different ways to transcend the repeated cycle of birth and death. Krishna explained the path of action, the path of devotion, and the path of knowledge. He assured Arjuna that these different paths are all viable ways to achieve salvation.

Main Subgroups

The major Hindu subgroups are organized around deities. Hinduism is old enough to have several layers of deities. The deities honored with hymns of praise in the Vedas are largely irrelevant to today's Hindu practice, although they appear as minor characters in mythology. Shaktas worship the Goddess in her different forms. Some forms of the Goddess are wives and consorts of male gods. Some are independent, linked to no particular god. What all forms of the Goddess have in common is Shakti, divine power. Shaivas (sometimes called Shaivites) worship the god Shiva, his wife Parvati, and their children Ganesha and Skanda. Vaishnavas (sometimes called Vaishnavites), worship the god Vishnu, his wife Lakshmi, and his ten avatars or incarnations. Rama, who once lived on earth as a king in North India, is celebrated in the Ramayana epic. Another incarnation of Vishnu is Krishna, venerated as a mischievous child, beautiful young man, and wise adult. Legends about the deities are found in the *Puranas*, a wide-ranging category of scripture that dates as early as the third century CE and as late as the fourteenth.

Practices

Family and home life play a vital role in Hinduism. Most Hindu families have shrines at home. Older people perform rituals for the family. It's common for the oldest woman in a household to offer daily puja (worship) ceremonies in the home shrine. Typically this is done every morning and evening. A puja might include chanting sacred mantras, meditation, scriptural recitation, and the waving of a lighted oil lamp. That last item, called arti, is a ritual gesture that dates to earlier times before shrines had electric lights; the lamp would allow the worshipper to see and be seen by the holy image.

Hindus mark transitions with lifecycle rituals. Of the 16 lifecycle rituals, families typically observe five: the birth ritual, the name-giving for a newborn child, the initiation with a sacred thread (for Brahmin and upper-caste boys), marriage, and cremation. Vow-taking is a common practice. One vows to venerate a particular god or goddess at his or her seat of worship at some future time. When seeking favor from the deities for initiatives like moving into a new home or starting a new job, it's common to invite priests to come to the house to perform special pujas.

Scriptures

Key scriptures for Hinduism include the following:

The Vedas
- *Rig Veda*
- *Yajur Veda*
- *Sama Veda*
- *Atharva Veda*

The Upanishads (major and minor)
Yoga Sutra
The Epics
- Ramayana
- Mahabharata

The Puranas
The Tantras

Festivals, Holidays, and Pilgrimages

Festivals and holy days fill the annual calendar of Hinduism. One hears the expression, "twelve months, thirteen festivals." Hindus use a lunar calendar, not the Gregorian calendar, to designate holy days. Hindu holidays vary from region to region. Indian public schools solve the problem of how to accommodate the many holidays and festivals observed in a multireligious nation by offering a menu of major and minor holidays and allowing students to select those for which they seek accommodation. Hindus living outside India find it necessary to structure holiday festivities around the conventions and laws of the host society, limiting festivals, for example, to weekends and daylight hours.

There are too many Hindu holidays to enumerate here. Major holidays include Diwali, the festival of lights (October/November). It is a five-day celebration of the victory of good over evil. Jains and Sikhs often celebrate Diwali. Navaratri,

Nine Nights (September/October) celebrates the power of the Goddess with folk dancing and the creation of large-scale temporary images. The night following Navaratri, called Dussehra, celebrates Rama's victory over the demon who abducted his wife. Holi (March) is a fun spring festival that involves throwing colored powders in a mood of joyous abandon. If possible, it's best to avoid scheduling major assignment due dates during these major celebrations. Many Hindus opt to visit family or take time off for observing.

The sacred powers of the physical environment play a role in Hinduism. Mountains draw pilgrims to ascend their heights and worship in caves, rock outcroppings, and other natural features. Rivers are said to embody the power of goddesses. Pilgrims who visit Rishikesh, a pilgrimage center located where the Ganges River emerges out of the Himalayan Mountains, flock to the riverside in the evening to watch small lamps float on the surface of the holy river. When a loved one dies and the body has been cremated, the ashes are often immersed in sacred rivers such as the Ganges. Here in America, the Ohio and the Mississippi Rivers tend to join the Ganges in the invocations of Hindu priests.

Common Misunderstandings, Stereotypes, and Classroom Concerns

Asian American students are stereotypically believed to be "smart" and "good at math." These stereotypes are described well by the "model minority myth," the idea that Asians as a group are highly intelligent, diligent, hardworking overachievers. As Alice Li explains in a TEDx talk, the model minority myth leads to fewer Asian Americans filing discrimination claims because they feel they would not be believed. The model minority myth proclaims that race is irrelevant to success in America: "just look at the Asians." By the same token, Asian American students often feel disinclined to speak up about racism they experience. The model minority myth suggests that Asian students will always succeed; they will be rewarded for their diligence and innate intelligence. In addition, the model minority myth exacerbates the divide between Asian Americans and other minorities, leading to Asian American students feeling isolated from other students of color who experience racism. The "perpetual foreigner syndrome" that stems from the underrepresentation of Asians in Western media has similar ramifications for Asian American students. It contributes to isolation. When educators assume that Asian American students are outsiders with a limited ability to fit into American institutions who will nonetheless thrive due to their work ethic and prodigious intellectual gifts, the "model minority myth" and "the perpetual foreigner syndrome" will lead many Hindu students to feel isolated from peers and school personnel.

Students from racially and religiously hybrid families often struggle to navigate a tight-rope of competing expectations about cultural authenticity. These expectations come from loved ones at home as well as peers and educators in school. Hindu students who are of mixed racial heritage or belong to nuclear families where one parent is non-Hindu can experience racism from their South Asian and Hindu extended families as well as from non-Hindu relatives. As the multiracial author Samira Mehta illustrates with anecdotes from her own extended family, it's often assumed that being racially mixed allows one to code-switch and easily adjust to being a part of more than one culture. But many times, the reverse is true for multiracial children. Mehta is the daughter of a South Asian father and North American mother. She has many physical features associated with South Asian people. Mehta describes herself as a child who preferred to avoid spicy Indian dishes. As she explains, many South Asian children whose palates are not yet used to chilies are given mildly spiced food specially cooked for them. As a child growing up in America, Mehta was sometimes treated by Indian American relatives as a harbinger of doom. Some of Samira Mehta's aunts and uncles could only see their bland-food-loving niece as an index of cultural defeat, an icon of all that is lost as American-born children of South Asian heritage assimilate to the insipid culinary norms typical of much standardized U.S. cuisine. Mehta's 2023 book, *The Racism of People Who Love You*, offers educators theoretical insights into the hybrid identities of many Asian American students, Hindus and non-Hindus.

Many non-Hindus approach Hinduism with the expectation that all Hindus are guided by a central scripture that articulates the essence of the religion. The *Bhagavad Gita* sits on bedside tables in many Hindu homes. If asked about the Hindu equivalent of the New Testament, many Hindus will offer the *Bhagavad Gita* as the book that captures what Hinduism has to offer. While many Hindus continue to value ritual forms as the connective tissue of the religion and would find the search for the religion's core beliefs pointless, Hindus living among Christians, Jews, and Muslims frequently adopt an approach to religion that emphasizes a single holy book and its associated creeds. A related trend can be seen in contemporary India, where a number of political parties grounded in Hinduism find it useful to present Hinduism in tight, doctrine-centered formulations that link Vedic wisdom to contemporary science. These groups are described by scholars of Hinduism with the catch-all term "Hindu right," since these groups tend to be socially and politically conservative.

Boundaries between religions of India may be more porous than some educators (and some students' family members) expect. Educators might thus be wary of assuming that a student's Hindu identity excludes other religious identities. Jains worship along with Hindus in many American temples, especially where the population of South Asian Americans is too low to support separate temples. But even in India, some Hindus visit shrines frequented by Muslims, Sikhs, and other non-Hindu groups, making offerings there for health, fertility, and wealth. Similarly, subgroups within the Hindu fold have porous boundaries. Although many families will venerate the same deities, it's not uncommon to find more than one subgroup in a given household.

Educators should be wary of common stereotypes of Hindu cultural practices that have emerged due to selective knowledge of the practices of one caste group or one regional form of Hinduism. For example, vegetarianism and avoiding the consumption of beef are ubiquitous stereotypes. Almost every

American knows the phrase "holy cow." Many Americans assume that it summarizes an essential way of being religious for all Hindus: that meat should not be eaten, that cows are to be protected, and that beef in particular is never to be eaten. In reality, over two-thirds of India's population eats meat; almost one-fifth eats beef. There are those who belong to meat-eating castes (such as Dalits/Bahujans) who don't actually eat much meat because they cannot afford it. But for these communities, meat-eating in no way violates their moral code. The holy cow stereotype is grounded in very recent history. The cow came to be deployed as a symbol of Hindu identity in the modern period, partly in response to the beef-heavy diet of British civil servants who occupied India during the colonial period. A beef-free diet was important to some Hindu nationalists who fought for India to become an independent nation free from British hegemony. The relatively recent vintage of the idea of cow-protection and the fact that beef would have been eaten during Vedic rituals complicates the idea that Hindus are vegetarians who abhor beef-eating.

Finally, it is very common in America to hear yoga described as a Hindu practice. While the term yoga occurs in ancient Hindu scripture, the series of gymnastic-style yogic postures seen in contemporary American yoga studios is quite different from the ethical and meditative program spoken of the *Yoga Sutra* of Patanjali, a key text for the philosophical school of yoga that centered on disciplining the mind and body through practices like moral training and breath control. Many American Hindus are baffled by the assumption that they have mastered the yogic postures taught in contemporary American yoga studios, although they may be proud to acknowledge the role that scriptures like the *Yoga Sutra* have provided for contemporary yoga practice.

Culturally Responsive Pedagogy

Hindus value ritual gestures, memorization, scriptural learning, and improvisational storytelling. These values constitute great assets in a classroom. Consider developing the following assignments and activities if you have a lot of Hindu students and want to see your Hindu students shine. You might develop some games or other ritualized modes of participation that enable each student to participate in a clearly defined way (especially helpful if one of your classes is a bit chaotic and participation happens too randomly for learning to take place). While not every Hindu student comes from a home where time is structured by rituals, some of your students might come from such a home and be well-versed in ritual gestures. Do you need to teach material that simply needs to be learned by rote? Some Hindu students may come from homes where feats of memorization are common, especially if the students have grown up in India and are of Brahmin heritage. Such students will shine when memorization is what's needed. But in a classroom that's been stultified by too much focus on testing and too much memorization, you might create assignments that amplify your students' creative capacities. Consider developing ways for students to create narratives that will make imparting and retaining information fun and easy. Almost every Hindu child learns scripture through storytelling. A good bit of the religion is learned while sitting in the arms of parents and grandparents, hearing recitations of stories from beloved epics such as the Ramayana or the Mahabharata. Each retelling of these epics is an improvisational, creative act. Local languages are used; local places are incorporated into the stories. Sometimes storytellers even place the people in their audience in the story, generating hyperlocal versions of the mythic stories they're telling that delight children and adults alike. If you develop assignments that highlight the creative imagination, it's likely that your Hindu students will shine.

Note

1   U.S. States by Population of Hindus, https://www.worldatlas.com/articles/us-states-by-population-of-hindus.html.

Further Reading and Resources

Doniger, Wendy. *The Hindus: An Alternative History*. New York: Penguin, 2009.

Doniger, Wendy. *On Hinduism*. New York and London: Oxford University Press, 2014.

Flueckiger, Joyce Burkhalter. *Everyday Hinduism*. Malden, MA: Wiley-Blackwell, 2015.

Fuller, Christopher J. *The Camphor Flame: Popular Hinduism and Society in India*. Princeton, NJ: Princeton University Press, 1992.

Knott, Kim. *Hinduism: A Very Short Introduction*. New York and London: Oxford University Press, 2016.

Li, Alice. "Why Asian Americans Are Not the Model Minority." TEDx Talks. Vanderbilt University. https://www.youtube.com/watch?v=87QkjfUEbz4

Mehta, Samira. *The Racism of People Who Love You*. Boston, MA: Beacon Press, 2023.

Rodrigues, Hillary P. *Introducing Hinduism*. New York and London: Routledge, 2006.

Sharma, Arvind. *Modern Hindu Thought: The Essential Texts*. New Delhi and New York, 2002.

Staples, James. *Sacred Cows and Chicken Manchurian: The Everyday Politics of Eating Meat in India*. Seattle: University of Washington Press, 2020.

27

Hinduism: Shaiva

> A Hindu woman in Pittsburgh fasts every Monday. She eats no food except for fruits and drinks only water and juice. If asked, she would explain that this day of the week is sacred to Shiva, the supreme being who takes the form of a yogi or ascetic who dwells in the Himalayas and is responsible for ending the universe when it has deteriorated over the centuries and is no longer a supportive environment for righteous living.

Introduction

The Shaiva denomination of Hinduism is the second largest, constituting about 25% of the Hindu population. However, given the centrality of goddesses associated with Shiva who are central to Shakta Hindu devotion, practices oriented to deities in the Shaiva family play a larger role in Hindu devotional life than one might expect from a sector of 25%.

Historical Overview

Shiva appears in the Vedas, the earliest layer of Hindu scripture, but he is not a central figure of devotion in this body of literature.

During the first millennium of the Common Era, devotion to Shiva became commonplace and elaborate theologies about Shiva's cosmic role developed.

Festivals, Holidays, and Pilgrimages

Maha Shivaratri is a major holiday centering on Lord Shiva. The name of this festival translates as "The Great Night of Shiva." Fasting, feasting, and gift-giving are all part of this festival.

Further Reading and Resources

Pattanaik Devadutt. *Shiva: An Introduction.* Mumbai: Vakils, Feffer and Simons Ltd., 1997.

Vanamali, Cēkkilār. *Shiva: Stories and Teachings from the Shiva Mahapurana.* Rochester, VT: Inner Traditions, 2013.

28

Hinduism: Shakta

> A family in Kolkata spends the evening touring their neighborhood, viewing large enclosures that their neighbors have erected in order to display large statues of Kali, the goddess who defeats evil and defends the innocent. Neighbors compete with one another to create the biggest, most spectacular displays.

Introduction

Shakti, the idea of the divine feminine, is one of the most central concepts of the Hindu tradition. Shakti is responsible for the universe's creation, maintenance, and destruction. Shakti takes many forms, including unmarried warrior goddesses like Kali and goddesses who are spouses of consorts of male deities.

Historical Overview

While goddesses are mentioned in the Vedas, the earliest layer of Hindu scripture, they are not mentioned as often as male deities in their body of literature. By the third or fourth century of the Common Era, however, the veneration of female forms of deity has become commonplace.

DOI: 10.4324/9781003405894-28

Practices

Animal sacrifices are offered to goddesses in some parts of South Asia. Sometimes a goat or water buffalo is sacrificed. Sometimes a vegetable substitute is offered. Venerating images of female deities is a common form of worship. This can be done at home, in a temple, or in a natural setting such as a rock outcropping that is said to be the seat of the goddess. Rivers are also an important locus of worship. Rivers are said to embody the power of goddesses. Pilgrims flock to the sacred city of Rishikesh, a pilgrimage center located where the Ganges River emerges out of the Himalayan mountains, in order to spend time touring temples during the day and visiting the riverside in the evenings.

Festivals, Holidays, and Pilgrimages

During the festival of Navaratri, or "Nine Nights" (September/October), Hindus celebrate the power of the goddess with folk dancing and the creation of large-scale temporary images.

Further Reading and Resources

Erndle, Kathleen. *Victory to the Mother: The Hindu Goddess of Northwest India in Myth, Ritual, and Symbol*. New York: Oxford University Press, 1993.

Chitgopekar, Nilima, and Shashi Tharoor. *Shakti: An Exploration of the Divine* (first American ed.). London: DK, 2022.

29

Hinduism: Vaishnava

> A suburban Hindu family drives to a Hindu temple in Houston to join a special musical event called a *kirtan*. In kirtan gatherings, the audience sings tales about the various deities. In the case of this Vaishnava temple, the kirtan focuses on songs about forms of Vishnu. There is a lead singer who introduces a song and the audience sings back in a call-and-response manner. The songs can last from 10 to 30 minutes each and there is reflective silence at the end of each song rather than clapping.

Introduction

The Vaishnava denomination of Hinduism is the largest, constituting about 67.6% of the Hindu population.[1] Vaishnavas are a diverse group of worshippers. The central deity Vishnu is said to take many forms, each needed to overcome a particular demonic opponent. Some of the forms are human, others are animals, and others still are a hybrid of human and animal. In addition to the diversity of distinctive ways of worshipping the many forms of the deity, there is also considerable regional diversity. In some regions, Vishnu's iconography is quite unique.

Historical Overview

Vishnu appears in the Vedas, the earliest layer of Hindu scripture, but he is not a central figure of devotion in this body of literature. During the first millennium of the Common Era devotion to Vishnu became commonplace. In the early centuries of the second millennium of the Common era, Vaishnavas contributed to a new movement of devotionalism that stressed the bonds of love that unite the human devotee and the deity.

Festivals, Holidays, and Pilgrimages

In North and South India, the holy day of Ekadasi is dedicated to Vishnu and is celebrated by fasting. Ekadasi occurs on the 11th day of each fortnight; grains are especially avoided.

Note

1   Johnson, Todd M., and Brian J. Grim, *The World's Religions in Figures: An Introduction to International Religious Demography*. Hoboken, NJ: John Wiley & Sons, 2013, p. 400.

Further Reading and Resources

Sara Black Brown. "From Meditation to Bliss: Achieving the Heights of Progressive Spiritual Energy through Kirtan Singing in American Gaudiya Vaishnava Hinduism." *Religions*, vol. 12, no. 8, 2021, p. 600.
Flood, Gavin. *An Introduction to Hinduism*. Cambridge, UK: Cambridge University Press, 1996.

30

Islam: Overview

> A family from Dearborn, Michigan, boards a plane in Saudi Arabia bound for Detroit. They are on their way back from a pilgrimage where they stood shoulder-to-shoulder with Muslims from all over the world. Muslim pilgrims who are in good health and have sufficient funds, like this family, try to go to Mecca at least once in their lives to visit the hometown of Muhammad, the prophet who established Islam. In Mecca, Muslim pilgrims celebrate not only events in the life of Muhammad and his family, but also older prophets like Abraham. Like many Muslims who have gone on the Hajj, chances are good that this American family regards their time in Mecca as a life-changing experience. The Hajj requires exertion and austerity, but it brings a powerful sense of unity as one visits holy places in the company of Muslims of all nationalities and ethnicities.

Introduction

2022 estimates suggest that Islam has some 1.97 billion adherents, representing 25% of the world's population.[1] This makes Islam the second largest religious group in the world. Islam is the third largest religion in the United States.[2] Muslims (those who practice Islam) living in the United States include immigrants from a wide range of countries and well as native-born converts. Islam is a pluralistic mosaic, not a monolith. It is a multicultural religion with a huge geographical span. With Muslims living in diverse cultures from the west coast of Africa all the way to Southeast Asia, it's clear that all Muslims could not possibly dress the same way and practice rituals in the same way. In Malaysia, a Muslim woman may spend time with others at a Muslim festival listening to gamelan music, wearing a light kerchief on her head. On the other side of the world, a festive gathering may look very different. With two major sects, practitioners on every continent, and 55 Muslim-majority countries, this is a religion that presents a lot of internal diversity. Religious obligations vary, including what is meant by obligatory prayer, almsgiving, and fasting. The major sects of Islam are Sunni and Shia. Sunni Muslims constitute the largest Muslim group. Sunni Muslims follow the teachings and practices of the Prophet Muhammad and rely on the Qur'an and Hadith (traditions of the Prophet) as their primary sources of guidance. Shia Muslims constitute a significant minority of the world Muslim population. They adhere to the teachings of the Prophet Muhammad and his family, particularly Muhammad's cousin and son-in-law, Imam Ali, and his descendants. There is also Sufism, a mystical set of practices within Islam that are sometimes mistakenly described as a separate sect of the religion. In the UnitedStates, migrants from all 55 countries and their descendants live in a society where the major sects of Islam are well represented. America is, in fact, home to the most diverse Muslim population in the world. But much depends on which part of the country you explore. In some parts of the United States, you will rarely see a Muslim, while in other parts there are huge Muslim enclaves. New York and New Jersey are home to many Muslims. Michigan also has a huge Muslim population. Dearborn, a suburb of Detroit, has the largest population of Muslims in America.

Historical Overview

Islam is often categorized as an Abrahamic religion – a religion that traces its roots back to the Biblical patriarch Abraham. Abraham was a prophet revered by Jews and Christians as the man who brought monotheism to humanity. Abraham made a covenant with God that he and his people would worship no other deities. God promised that in return, Abraham's line would flourish. From the example of Abraham and other shared prophets, the connections among the three Abrahamic religions of Judaism, Christianity, and Islam are clear. Muslims take the revered figures of Judaism and Christianity as prophets and find sustenance in the narratives of the Hebrew Bible and the New Testament. Muslims view Muhammad as the final prophet in a line of monotheistic prophets shared by these other religions.

The Prophet Muhammad was born around 570 of the Common Era. Muhammad ibn Abdullah was orphaned at an early age. As a young man, he led trade caravans for a wealthy widow named Khadija. Khadija was so impressed with his character that she asked Muhammad to marry her. Khadija gave Muhammad comfort when he began receiving the revelations that are the basis of the Qur'an, the Muslim holy book. These revelations centered on the God worshipped by Jews and Christians, known in Arabic as *Allah*. Muhammad's insistence on monotheism and resistance to the worship of pagan deities prominent in his hometown led to antipathy with local tribes. Eventually Muhammad and his followers relocated to a city now known as Medina. With vigorous support in Medina, the religion began to spread. Without any formal body of leadership, Islam nevertheless spread rapidly into many regions. Within a few centuries of the death of Muhammad, Islam had spread throughout the Middle East as well as into North Africa and the Iberian Peninsula (today's Spain). Muslims eventually set up dynasties in India and formed the vast Ottoman dynasty, centered in Turkey. The Islamic world is geographically vast, with Muslim-majority countries tracing the globe from Western Africa to Southeast Asia and with significant Muslim populations in Europe and North America.

Scripture and Other Sources of Guidance

The majority of Muslims regard the Qur'an as the word of God, dictated to Muhammad without human editing. In addition to the revelation contained in the Qur'an, Muslims take guidance on how to live from anecdotes about things that Muhammad said and did (known as Hadiths, "Traditions"). Another source of guidance is Islamic law or Shari'a. Shari'a includes customs and rituals as well as formal religious law. Shari'a plays a dual role of helping humans achieve salvation and maintaining the kind of society that supports pious behavior. There are five schools of Islamic law, with different schools dominant in different geographical areas. Obligations include prayer, almsgiving, and fasting.

Worship

The core practices – the so-called pillars of Islam – are key acts of worship that elevate a person's faith in God and promote virtue. Sunni Muslims regard five practices as central to the life of a Muslim. Shia Muslims, depending on the sect, hold that there are seven or ten such central practices.

The Five Pillars:

1. Shahada, the declaration of faith. To be a Muslim is to submit to God. This is encapsulated in the Arabic phrase, "La ilaha illa Allah, Muhammadun rasul Allah," which means "There is no deity worthy of worship except Allah, and Muhammad is the Messenger of Allah." A person who joins the religion of Islam indicates adherence by reciting the formula.
2. Salat, the prayer ritual, performed as often as five times a day. The specific times of the day are dawn (Fajr), noon (Dhuhr), afternoon (Asr), evening (Maghrib), and night (Isha). Shia Muslims pray as often as three times a day; Sunni Muslims pray as often as five times a day. Prayers occur at intervals based on the movement of the sun. Times for prayer thus vary based on location and season. While praying, Muslims face toward Mecca. Once prayer begins, it should not be interrupted.
3. Zakat, charity. It's common to give 2.5% of one's wealth on an annual basis.

4. Sawm, fasting. Ramadan is a month-long period that celebrates the month when Muhammad received the first of the revelations that make up the Qur'an. It is the ninth month of the Islamic lunar calendar. Many Muslims abstain from food and water from sunrise to sunset and avoid sexual intimacy during Ramadan. Not everyone is expected to fast, including those who are unwell, children who have not reached puberty, elderly adults, and women who are pregnant, lactating, or menstruating. For those who can abstain from eating, drinking, and sex, the Ramadan holiday offers a taste of self-discipline, an elevated sense of reverence for God, and a greater sense of empathy for those who regularly go hungry. Because the holiday involves self-discipline and giving up comforts, Ramadan can be described as "Easter on steroids." It is a time when people give up creature comforts. But it is also a time of feasting, with special meals before sunrise and after sunset. For children in North America, Ramadan can also be the equivalent of Christmas. Special foods, decorations, and presents mark the holiday as a festive one.
5. Hajj, pilgrimage to the city of Mecca, where the Prophet Muhammad was born. It is required once in a lifetime if one can afford to go and if one is physically able to make the pilgrimage. Pilgrims move around the landscape in Mecca and connect with transformative events of the past, including events associated with prophets such as Abraham. Special white clothing is worn, clothing that flattens distinctions between different groups. In the image below, a small group of youthful pilgrims wear white cotton robes while circling the Kaaba (a shrine that houses a meteor) in 2023. Muslims from around the world mingle with one another and join together in performing rituals on a massive scale. Before the pandemic reduced the number of pilgrims, the Hajj typically brought over two million pilgrims together. Muslims from all over the world make tremendous sacrifices to experience unity and equality while walking in the footsteps of the

prophets. The 2023 Hajj occurred during a heat wave, with daytime high temperatures hovering around 116 degrees Fahrenheit. Most of the activities take place outdoors with little if any shade. But like undergraduates who voluntarily suffer fraternity and sorority initiations in U.S. college settings, pilgrims sense that suffering with a group promotes bonding and solidarity. Pilgrims on the Hajj endure discomfort together while wiping away sin and basking in devotion to God.

Holidays and Festivals

- Ramadan, a month-long dawn-to-dust fast that celebrates the descent of the Qur'an, times vary based on lunar calendar.
- Eid al-Fitr, celebrates the end of the Ramadan fast, times vary based on lunar calendar. The holiday lasts for 1–3 days, depending on country. Many Muslims will attend morning prayers during Eid al-Fitr. Congregational prayer, feasting, and visiting family are all part of the holiday.
- Eid al-Adha, a four-day holiday in honor of the sacrifice of Abraham.
- Fridays are the holiest days of the week. Congregational prayer is held in mosques and special meals are eaten at home.

Common Misunderstandings, Stereotypes, and Classroom Concerns

Daily prayer is, as is well known, a common marker of piety. Shia Muslims pray three times a day; Sunni Muslims pray five times a day. Prayers occur at intervals based on the movement of the sun. Thus times for prayer vary based on location and season. The spaces set aside for prayer must allow for preliminary washing (mouths, nose, ears, hands, and forearms) and for various positions during prayer, such as standing, bending, kneeling, and prostration. While praying, Muslims face toward Mecca. Once s/he begins praying, a Muslim will avoid interrupting her prayer.

The diet prescribed for Muslims prohibits meat that has not been slaughtered according to Islamic custom and has significant amounts of blood in it. In addition, Muslims are to avoid pork and to eat in moderation. Many Muslims avoid alcohol, tobacco, and recreational drugs.

For those in charge of procuring food for the school cafeteria, vegetarian food should be provided for students associated with the Nation of Islam. For other Muslim students, vegetarian or kosher food may be served if halal foods (meat prepared according to Muslim law) are not available. Since pork is prohibited for all Muslims, do not serve Muslim students products like gelatin that contain byproducts from pigs. School nurses should be aware that certain medications containing alcohol should be avoided.

Care must be taken not to touch the Qur'an, nor to leave it on the floor or to put anything on top of the holy book. Washing is required before touching the Qur'an. If it's necessary to handle the Qur'an, one can wrap it up in a clean cloth to show respect for its sacred state.

Ramadan is a time of special concern for student athletes. Since Muslims abstain from hydration during daylight hours, fasting athletes should be monitored for signs of dehydration. They should also take care when breaking the fast to eat foods that metabolize slowly. Carbohydrates are recommended; high sugar content foods are not recommended. Although Muslims avoid medications when fasting, inhalers, eye drops, and ear drops are permitted during daytime hours.

Modesty stands out among the virtues that Muslims seek to practice. This can mean different things to different Muslims, but at minimum means that students should be asked about the arrangements that make them uncomfortable. In some cases, students will prefer same-sex groups for class activities. Men should be allowed to remain covered between the knees and the navel. Women's coverings vary considerably based on different Muslim cultures, different households, and different individual preferences. Some Muslim women and girls dress in the same manner as their non-Muslim peers. They do not wear head coverings or special garments. Some Muslim women and girls cover their heads and chests. Some wear head coverings that ensure that no hair shows. Others are less concerned about concealing hair. Some Muslim women and girls strive to cover every part of their bodies except their hands and face.

Muslim students are likely to respond well to classroom activities that reward patience, since patience is believed to be a strong marker of faith in God. Open-ended inquiry where the results are uncertain may be more palatable to Muslim students than some other students. Muslims may be more comfortable with uncertainty due to the habit of allowing God's will to prevail in everyday life. The phrase "in sha Allah" ("by God's will") is a constant refrain for many Muslims, indicating the virtue of leaving important things up to God's will.

Notes

1 Lipka, Michael and Conrad Hackett, "Why Muslims Are the World's Fastest Growing Religious Group," Pew Research Center, 2017, https://www.pewresearch.org/short-reads/2017/04/06/why-muslims-are-the-worlds-fastest-growing-religious-group/
2 Muhammad, Basheer, "New Estimates Show U.S. Muslim Population Continues to Grow," Pew Research Center, 2018, https://www.pewresearch.org/short-reads/2018/01/03/new-estimates-show-u-s-muslim-population-continues-to-grow/

Further Reading and Resources

Bucar, Liz. *The Islamic Veil: A Beginners Guide*. London: One World, 2012.
Curtis, Edward E. *The Practice of Islam in America: An Introduction*. New York: New York University Press, 2017.
Douglass, S. L., and R. E. Dunn. "Interpreting Islam in American Schools." *The ANNALS of the American Academy of Political and Social Science*, vol. 588, no. 1, 2003, pp. 52–72.

Fordson: Faith, Fasting, Football. North Shore Films LLC, 2011.
Gibson, Dawn-Marie. *A History of the Nation of Islam: Race, Islam, and the Quest for Freedom.* Westport, CT: Praeger, 2012.
Hajj. PBS, 2014.
Inside Islam: What a Billion Muslims Really Think. Unity Productions Foundation, 2009.
Islam: There Is No God But God. Ambrose Video, 1977.
Peek, Lori. "Becoming Muslim: The Development of a Religious Identity." *Sociology of Religion*, vol. 66, no. 3, 2005, pp. 215–242.
Ruthven, Malise. *Islam: A Very Short Introduction* (Very Short Introductions). New York: Oxford University Press, 2012.
What Is Islam? TMW Media, 2013.

31

Islam: The Nation of Islam

> A family in Chicago gathers around the dinner table and takes a serving of bean pie. This dish was created as an alternative to sweet potato pie – a food commonly eaten by enslaved Black Americans living on plantations in the South.

Historical Overview

The Nation of Islam is an American form of Islam that had its beginnings in the 1930s. It arose primarily in Chicago and Detroit, with a strong following among Blacks who had relocated to cities in the North from the rural South during the Great Migration. W.D. Fard (also known as Wallace Fard Muhammad) and his disciple Elijah Muhammad led the organization with a message of Black unity and the superiority of the Black race. Adherents of the early Nation of Islam worked for economic self-sufficiency as well as separation from White society. Elijah Muhammad taught that Blacks had developed the first advanced civilization but that whites had taken over, enslaved Blacks, and brought about the loss of Black identity and religion. Leaders of the Nation of Islam emphasized historical connections to powerful Muslim communities in Africa. Leaders encouraged adherents to do for self, cultivate their own interests, eat and live in a clean manner, and avoid intermarriage with Whites.

Not only has the Nation of Islam consistently worked to lift up marginalized members of the U.S. Black community, but it has also sought to improve the lives of oppressed peoples in other parts of the world. It has been a vocal critic of U.S. imperialism. For example, when many Americans were drafted to fight in the Vietnam War in the twentieth century, Nation of Islam leaders such as Malcolm X spoke out against U.S. involvement in this war and drew attention to the plight of innocent Southeast Asian civilians caught up in the conflict.

After the death of Elijah Muhammad, the Nation of Islam underwent changes in direction. Wareeth Deen Muhammad succeeded his father and turned the organization toward Sunni Islamic practices. Louis Farrakhan disagreed with the new direction of the organization and led a movement to revive earlier Nation of Islam goals and practices.

Holidays, Worship, and Key Practices

Nation of Islam adherents often take new names if their given names were inherited from slave owners. Adherents lead disciplined lives. They believe in eating moderately and fasting often. Nation of Islam adherents avoid a long list of foods, especially those typical of what enslaved people ate on American plantations, such as catfish and collard greens. Vegetarianism is encouraged. Alcohol and tobacco are to be avoided. During the month of December, Nation of Islam adherents fast during daylight hours. Male members of the Nation dress conservatively, wearing suits with ties or bowties and cutting their hair short. Women dress modestly and avoid wearing trousers. Women have the option of wearing head coverings.

Common Misunderstandings, Stereotypes, and Classroom Concerns

Students with families that belong to the Nation of Islam bear a double burden – they are not just subject to the racism that is pervasive in American society, but they must also deal with the stereotypes associated with the Nation of Islam. Care should be taken to avoid generalizations and to redirect conversations that rely on stereotypes. If some students are put off by the Nation of Islam's separatism and its critique of imperialism, it can be pointed out that while the Nation has used revolutionary rhetoric, it has avoided war and violence.

Culturally Responsive Pedagogy

Students who adhere to the Nation of Islam will likely thrive when engaged in assignments that stress equality and social justice. To counter stereotypes that link the Nation of Islam with violence, an assignment that focuses on the outsize role of the Nation of Islam as a critic of U.S. efforts to escalate the conflict in Vietnam could be useful.

Further Reading and Resources

Curtis, Edward IV. *Islam in Black America: Identity, Liberation, and Difference in African-American Islamic Thought.* Albany, NY: State University of New York Press, 2002.

White, Vibert L., Jr. *Inside the Nation of Islam: A Historical and Personal Testimony of a Black Muslim.* Gainesville, FL: University Press of Florida, 2001.

32

Islam: Shia

> A Shia family of Pakistani origin living in Detroit attends a mourning gathering that reminds them of the loss of early community leaders.

Introduction

Shia Muslims make up 10%–13% of Muslims in the world.[1] They adhere to the teachings of the Prophet Muhammad and his family, particularly Muhammad's cousin and son-in-law, Imam Ali, and his descendants, who constitute a line of leaders called Imams. Iran, Iraq, Azerbaijan, and Bahrain are Shia majority countries. There are also significant numbers of Shia Muslims in India and Pakistan. The Shia community consists of various sub-sects, such as Twelvers (the largest group), Ismailis, and Zaydis.

Sunni and Shia prayer differs in minor details. Sunnis generally cross their arms in prayer, while Shia Muslims stand with their arms hanging on each side. Shia Muslims also recite an additional short prayer that Sunnis generally omit. Shia Muslims also combine some of the five daily prayers.

Holidays, Festivals, and Worship

Some holidays are celebrated in different ways, depending on what form of Islam one adheres to. Such is the case with Muharram, the first month of the Islamic year. Fighting has traditionally been prohibited during this month. The day of Ashura, the 10th day of the month, holds different significance according to the sect one follows. Sunnis celebrate Ashura as the day that Moses led his people out of Egypt, crossing the Red Sea. Shias mourn the day in a more solemn manner as they recall the martyrdom of Imam Hussain, the grandson of Prophet Muhammad and his companions, who died at the Battle of Karbala. Mourning processions, recitations of poetry and hymns, and (in some communities) self-flagellation are common.

Note

1   Wikipedia: Islam by Country, https://en.wikipedia.org/wiki/Islam_by_country

Further Reading and Resources

Harney, John. "How Do Sunni and Shia Islam Differ?" *The New York Times* (2016): A6.

Hazleton, Lesley. *After the Prophet: The Epic Story of the Shia-Sunni Split in Islam* (1st ed.). New York City: Doubleday, 2009.

33

Islam: Sunni

> A married couple from Houston, Texas, discuss their finances and determine the dollar amount they will offer as a charity in the coming year.

Introduction

Sunni Muslims constitute the largest sect of Islam. A 87%–90% of Muslims belong to this group.[1] Sunni Muslims follow the teachings and practices of the Prophet Muhammad and rely on the Qur'an and Hadith (traditions of the Prophet) as their primary sources of guidance.

Historical Overview

See the chapter titled "Islam: Overview" and look for the heading "Historical Overview."

Scripture and Other Sources of Guidance

See the chapter titled "Islam: Overview" and look for the heading "Historical Overview."

Worship

When textbooks that cover Islam teach about the five pillars, they are in fact presenting what Sunni Muslims regard as central rather than what is universal for all Muslims. Sunnis regard five practices as central to the life of a Muslim, but Shia Muslims, depending on the sect, hold that there are seven or ten such central practices.

Holidays and Festivals

See **Islam Overview: Holidays and Festivals**

Common Misunderstandings, Stereotypes, and Classroom Concerns

See **Islam: Common Misunderstandings, Stereotypes, and Classroom Concerns**

Note

1   Bennett, Clifton, *Islamic Beliefs, Practices, and Cultures: Subdivisions within Islam*, Tarrytown, NJ: Marshall Cavendish Reference, 2010, p. 130.

Further Reading and Resources

Bucar, Liz. *The Islamic Veil: A Beginners Guide*. London: One World, 2012.
Curtis, Edward E. *The Practice of Islam in America: An Introduction*. New York City: New York University Press, 2017.
Gibson, Dawn-Marie. *A History of the Nation of Islam: Race, Islam, and the Quest for Freedom*. Westport, CT: Praeger, 2012.
Hajj. PBS, 2014.

Inside Islam: What a Billion Muslims Really Think. Washington, DC: Unity Productions Foundation, 2009.
Islam: There Is No God But God. Ambrose Video, 1977.
Ruthven, Malise. *Islam: A Very Short Introduction* (Very Short Introductions). Oxford, UK: Oxford University Press, 2012.
What Is Islam? TMW Media, 2013.

34

Jainism

> A pre-teen Jain girl goes to sing devotional songs with her aunt. She learns about Jain's conceptions of karma and the universe through the songs she sings and conversation with her aunt, who is deeply learned in scripture. Upon returning home, the girl and her aunt prepare festival foods for a show-and-tell assignment at school. In presenting hand-prepared vegetarian foods to her classmates, she is able to teach lessons about non-violence, the ethical connections that humans have to the more-than-human souls that inhabit the Jain universe, and to explain how Jains conceive the path to liberation.

Introduction

Jainism is a fascinating religion that is practiced by relatively few people. As of 2023, between three and four million followers of the Jain religion were recorded as living in India; about 150,000 Jains live outside India.[1] Adherents in India tend to be wealthier and more educated than their counterparts in other religions.

The Jain worldview is essentially atheistic. It centers on the lives of omniscient saints who have escaped the cycle of birth and death and forged a path for others to follow. In the past, the saints are said to have been born in numerous times and places, among gods, animals, human beings and other birth realms.

As they reach the end of their reincarnation journey, the saints live lives of self-discipline. Some adherents of the religion follow the example of saints and live as monks and nuns. Others live as laypeople who support monastics. The principle of non-violence is central to Jain's religious practice. Jains believe that all living beings have souls. Hence causing harm to any of these beings is wrong. Jains follow a strict vegetarian diet in order to avoid harming sentient beings. They avoid eating root vegetables; by uprooting them, the entire plant dies.

Holidays and Festivals

Mahavir Jayanti (celebrated in March or April) is a central festival in this religion. It celebrates the birth of Mahavira, the twenty-fourth and last supreme preacher of the present cosmic cycle. Statues of Mahavira are anointed with oil and carried in procession to recognize Mahavira's key role in the religion. Jains also celebrate Diwali or Deepawali, a Hindu festival that adherents of other religions in India also find meaningful. Diwali is celebrated with gift exchanges, fireworks, and festive lights.

Classroom Concerns, Stereotypes

Asian American students are stereotypically believed to be "smart" and "good at math." These stereotypes are described well by the "model minority myth," the idea that Asians as a group are highly intelligent, diligent, hardworking overachievers. As Alice Li explains in a TEDx talk, the model minority myth leads to fewer Asian Americans filing discrimination claims because they feel they would not be believed. The model minority myth proclaims that race is irrelevant to success in America: "just look at the Asians." By the same token, Asian American students often feel disinclined to speak up about the racism they experience. The model minority myth suggests that Asian students will always succeed; they will be rewarded for their diligence and innate intelligence. In addition, the model minority myth exacerbates the divide between Asian Americans and other minorities, leading to Asian American students feeling isolated from other students of color who experience racism. The "perpetual foreigner syndrome" that stems from the underrepresentation of Asians in Western media has similar ramifications for Asian American students. It contributes to isolation. When educators assume that Asian American students are outsiders with a limited ability to fit into American institutions who will nonetheless thrive due to their work ethic and prodigious intellectual gifts, the "model minority myth" and "the perpetual foreigner syndrome" will lead many Jain students to feel isolated from peers and school personnel.

Note

1 World Population Review, https://worldpopulationreview.com/country-rankings/jain-population-by-country.

Further Reading and Resources

Balbir, Nalini. *Gender and Jainism*. Encyclopedia of Religion, Detroit: MacMillan Press, 2005.
Fohr, Sherry. *Jainism: A Guide for the Perplexed*. London: Bloomsbury, 2014.
Li, Alice. "Why Asian Americans Are Not the Model Minority." *TEDx Talks*. Vanderbilt University. https://www.youtube.com/watch?v=87QkjfUEbz4
Long, Jeffrey. *Jainism: An Introduction*. London: I.B.Tauris, 2009.

35

Judaism: Overview

Membership

Since American Jews differ considerably about exactly what constitutes a Jew, it is difficult to give precise numbers. The best available for the early 2020s are:

Total Jewish population (including all who identify as Jewish in some way): 8,000,000 (2.4% of the total U.S. population).[1]

Terminology and History

Judaism designates the religion that originated among the Hebrew people in what is now the nation of Israel, and which has persisted to the present day in various shapes and sizes. In the nineteenth-century United States, tensions forming around questions of how to maintain continuity of traditions in the face of modernization led to organizational divisions among American Jewish groups. What had heretofore been a diffuse American community of many persuasions settled into distinct denominations, all sharing a common tradition but divided over what impact modern thought and society should play in the practice of tradition in a pluralistic society. The major strains of American Judaism are Orthodox, Reform, and Conservative.

The Jewish people are those who claim membership in a community descended from these early Hebrews. Many Jews who are not religiously observant, or who even regard themselves as agnostics or atheists, still regard themselves as Jewish in terms of their descent and continuing participation in Jewish life, especially in support for Israel.

Jewish culture is a mix of ancient tradition and adaptation to the "host cultures" among which Jews have lived over centuries of *diaspora* (scattering). In the United States, Jewish culture has varied from the Yiddish-speaking communities in New York City and other enclaves to the legacy of this now largely dispersed culture, expressed in linguistic quirks ("Yinglish," a Yiddish-accented form of English), and traditional foods such as pastrami, blintzes, and kugel sold in delicatessens. This culture has entered the broader American realm through mass media, from the films of Mel Brooks to the parodies of Adam Sandler to the novels of Philip Roth.

Worship and Ritual

Jewish worship is conducted weekly on the Sabbath (Shabbat), observed from sundown Friday to sundown Saturday at a synagogue. It is usually conducted by a *rabbi* (teacher). The service consists of reading from Hebrew scripture, prayers and, among many today, a sermon. Men traditionally don a skullcap known as a *yarmulke* (pronounced 'YAH-mah-kah') or *kippa*.

Scriptures

The core of Jewish worship is the *Torah* – Genesis, Exodus, Leviticus, Numbers, Deuteronomy – said by tradition to have been directly dictated to Moses by God. The entire Hebrew bible consists of the Torah plus the Prophets – Jeremiah, Isaiah, and the like – plus the "Writings," which consist of historical books like Chronicles and Kings, and other books in a variety of genres such as Daniel, an apocalyptic narrative. The Tanakh is supplemented by rabbinical interpretations and legal judgments contained in the *Midrash* and the *Talmud*.

Holidays and Festivals

Judaism has many holidays/holy days and festivals, the formal observance of which is largely restricted to the High Holy Days in the fall and Passover in the spring. The High Holy Days begin with Rosh Hashanah – the Jewish New Year – and end ten days later with Yom Kippur, the Day of Atonement. These "Days of Awe" are observed in the synagogue or temple and, in some ways like the Christian Lent, are a time for repentance in preparation for the coming of a new year.

Passover, the prototype for the Christian Easter, is family centered, and its celebration consists of the gathering of a ritualized meal commemorating the archetypal Jewish event, the Exodus from bondage in Egypt. The meal consists of the recitation of a special liturgy; the asking of traditional questions by children; and the eating of symbolic foods, such as unleavened bread and bitter herbs, evocative of the hasty exit from Egypt and the sufferings involved in this adventure.

An American innovation is the celebration of Hannukah each December, a previously rather minor holiday now emphasized as a Jewish alternative to Christmas. It is marked by the lighting of candles on a nine-branched *menorah* – candelabrum – in commemoration of the successful resistance in the second century B.C.E. by Judas Maccabeus and a small band of Israelis to Greek rule in the Holy Land. This heroic band's oil supply, no more than a day's worth, miraculously lasted for eight days symbolized by the menorah candles. (*Latkes*, potato pancakes deep-fried in oil, similarly evoke the oil motif.) More a folk festival than a solemn holy day, it emphasizes the role of children, who play games with a *dreidel* – a spinning top with Hebrew letters on each side – and receive gifts from "Uncle Max the Hanukkah Man," a playful Jewish version of Santa Claus. (Such gifts may be left under a "Hanukkah bush.")

NOTE: Hebrew words such as Hanukkah vary in spelling when rendered in the Roman alphabet, as in "Chanukkah," since there is no single English letter rendering the initial guttural sound represented as "H" or "CH."

Rites of passage include the bar mitzvah and bat mitzvah for adolescent boys and girls, whereby they gain adult status in their congregations. Jewish weddings include distinctive customs, such as the groom shattering a glass and the bridal couple standing beneath a *huppah* (canopy) during the ceremony. Intermarriage between Jews and Gentiles has become widespread in recent decades, and many rabbis refuse of officiate at such services. Deaths are marked by sitting shivah, the gathering of mourners with the family over several days, and by an anniversary candle-lighting, the *Yahrzeit* (year-time).

Common Misunderstandings, Stereotypes, and Classroom Concerns

For Jews, the term "Old Testament" as a synonym for "Hebrew scripture" is at worst offensive and at best an occasion for eye-rolling. "Hebrew scripture" and "Christian scripture" are preferable neutral terms.

Similarly, the abbreviations A.D. (*anno domini*, "the year of our Lord") and B.C. ("before Christ") are clearly Christian-centered and should be avoided in favor of C.E. ("the Common Era") and B.C.E. ("Before the Common Era"), although the use of A.D./B.C. is so deeply ingrained that it is difficult to change its usage.

The observance of Christmas in this country has become so much a part of a commercialized common culture as to have lost much of its religious meaning, but it can still be problematic if not subsumed into a more inclusive or secularized holiday celebration. In other words, no creches in the classroom.

Another issue, brought to the fore in the 2020s by international political developments, is that of Zionism. Zion is an ancient name for what is now Israel – the divinely ordained Jewish homeland – restored to nationhood in 1947 by the United Nations's mandate following the Holocaust – the extermination of some six million European Jews – during the Nazi regime during the 1930s and early 40s.

Current politics, in the United States and Israel, revolve around the question of whether opposition to the foreign and military policies of the nation of Israel can be construed as antisemitic. The main issue here is whether such opposition can be construed as antisemitic and anti-Zionist, or whether such policies can be criticized without denying the legitimacy of the Israeli state. The matter is further complicated by the unresolved question of whether Israel is a religious state, with ultra-Orthodox Jews (*Haredim*) granted control over religious matters as well as exemption from compulsory military service. (The latter has recently been rescinded.) These issues should be handled delicately.

Jews over the centuries have been plagued by stereotypes which still subsist in the American scene. These include physical characteristics such as the "Jewish nose," a feature by no means possessed by all Jews but shared by other Mediterranean peoples.

Antisemitism – animosity toward Jews – still perpetuates a certain sense of tension, especially in the context of relations between the United States and Israel and its conflicts with militant Islamic groups such as Hamas.

Stereotypes of Jews as uncouth and "pushy" arose from issues of rapid but imperfect assimilation and led to the imposition of "Jewish quotas" by Ivy League and other prestigious colleges beginning in the 1920s. With Jews later entering the professions in significant numbers, discrimination such as exclusion from gentile neighborhoods and social clubs has receded rapidly in recent decades.

A long-term concern for schools serving significant numbers of Jewish children has been the observance of dietary practices and major religious holidays. These matters should be settled on a local basis, and may include providing kosher alternatives to standard cafeteria fare and allowing for time off for major holidays. Schools or school districts with large Jewish populations often cancel classes on such days.

Probably the best way to counteract prejudice against Jewish students is through providing accurate information and open discussion about Jewish tradition appropriate to age level, perhaps using holidays and dietary practices as a springboard for defusing any negative sense of Jewish "otherness." Sensitivity to public controversies such as those involving Israel needs to be addressed openly, and verbal or physical violence must be actively discouraged. Visits to Jewish houses of worship and discussions with staff members could help "normalize" Jewish tradition and culture for students to whom it may be unfamiliar.

Note

1 United States Census 2020 data as reported by the Pew Research Center, https://www.pewresearch.org/religion/2021/05/11/the-size-of-the-u-s-jewish-population/.

Further Reading and Resources

Lippy, Charles H., and Peter W. Williams, eds. *Encyclopedia of Religion in America*. Washington, DC: CQ Press, 2010, "Judaism: Conservative," 1114–1119; "Judaism: Jewish Culture," 1120–1124; "Judaism: Jewish Identity," 1125–1132; "Judaism: Jewish Science," 1133–1134; "Judaism: Orthodox," 1135–1140; "Judaism: Reconstructionist," 1141–1143; "Judaism: Reform," 1144–1149; "Judaism: Sectarian Movements," 1150–1152; "Judaism: Secular," 1153–1157; "Judaism: Tradition and Heritage," 1158–1168.

Sarna, Jonathan D. *American Judaism: A History*. New Haven, CT: Yale University Press, 2005.

36

Judaism: Conservative

On March 18, 1922, Judith Kaplan became the first young woman in history to celebrate a Bat Mitzvah, a ritual acknowledging her coming of age as an adult member of the Jewish community. Prior to this, only boys could experience this rite of initiation, the Bar Mitzvah ("son of the covenant"). This ritual is old but not ancient, and is based on the Christian sacrament of confirmation. Ms. Kaplan, however, was no ordinary Jewish teenager. Her father, Mordecai Kaplan, was a rabbi responsible for an offshoot of the Conservative movement known as Reconstructionist Judaism, which emphasized, in his phrase, "Judaism as a Civilization" – a way of being Jewish that is more cultural rather than traditionally religious. Reform Jews later adopted the Bat Mitzvah as well, but Orthodox have refused innovations that accommodate an equal religious status for females.

Membership

Approximate membership for 2020

2,800,000 (35% of a total U.S. Jewish population of about 8,000,000)[1]

DOI: 10.4324/9781003405894-36

History

Conservative Judaism, a distinctively American movement, emerged early in the twentieth century as a middle way between what many Jews saw as the extremes of Orthodoxy and Reform. It adheres to Talmudic law as an authentic guide to practice, but maintains that the interpretation of tradition has to be reassessed periodically in favor of justice in contemporary situations. Thus, it permits the ordination of women and gays. Conservative Jews generally follow the kosher laws and other traditional practices. *Reconstructionism* is an offshoot of the Conservative movement, seeing Judaism more as a civilization than a religion with a personal God.

Worship and Ritual

See **Judaism Overview: Worship and Ritual**

Scriptures

See **Judaism Overview: Scriptures**

Holidays and Festivals

See **Judaism Overview: Holidays and Festivals**

Common Misunderstandings, Stereotypes, and Classroom Concerns

See **Judaism Overview: Common Misunderstandings, Stereotypes, and Classroom Concerns**

Note

1 Pew Research Center Report on the U.S. 2020 Census, https://www.pewresearch.org/religion/2021/05/11/jewish-americans-in-2020/.

Further Reading and Resources

Lippy, Charles H., and Peter W. Williams, eds. *Encyclopedia of Religion in America*. Washington, DC: CQ Press, 2010, "Judaism: Conservative," 1114–1119; "Judaism: Jewish Culture," 1120–1124; "Judaism: Jewish Identity," 1125–1132; "Judaism: Jewish Science," 1133–1134; "Judaism: Sectarian Movements," 1150–1152; "Judaism: Secular," 1153–1157; "Judaism: Tradition and Heritage," 1158–1168.

Sarna, Jonathan D. *American Judaism: A History*. New Haven, CT: Yale University Press, 2005.

37

Judaism: Orthodox

> If you happen to be strolling through midtown Manhattan, or are looking for the perfect diamond ring for that special occasion, you may find yourself on a stretch of 47th Street between 5th and 6th Avenues known as the "Diamond District." Ninety percent of American diamonds come through New York City, and most of those find their way to this block, where $400,000,000 of trade takes place each day. In addition to the glitter of the diamonds – it is said that the streets shine – one will see men dressed in black wearing forelocks – a variation on sideburns – and black clothing and hats. These are Orthodox Jews whose forebears fled Antwerp and Amsterdam at the beginning of World War II and vastly expanded the District with their presence and expertise. European Jews had for centuries dealt in diamonds since they frequently had to flee persecution on short notice, and diamonds were easily carried in their clothes.

Membership

Approximate U.S. membership for 2020–720,000 (6% of a total U.S. Jewish population of about 8,000,000)[1]

History and Terminology

In the beginning, all Judaism was Orthodox. In that beginning, in fact, "Judaism" didn't even exist as a word or concept. The forerunners of what we now call the Jewish people and their religion were the Hebrews, 12 Middle Eastern tribes who coalesced – as recounted in the books of Genesis and Exodus of the *Torah* – into a single entity with a common identity and set of religious practices. The terms "Judaism," "Jewish," and "Jews" are all derived from this people's residence in Greek-speaking Alexandria and Antioch in the two centuries or so before and after the coming of the Christian movement, when their scriptures were translated into Greek – the *Septuagint*. This was part of a wider phenomenon known as the *Diaspora*, when they were scattered from their homeland of Israel through successive conquests and had to adapt to life among the *gentiles* – non-Jews – as subordinates.

Jews who fled northward into Europe to avoid persecution or to follow economic opportunities became known as Ashkenazic Jews – *Ashkenazim* – while those who dispersed around the Mediterranean basin are called Sephardic – *Sephardim*. A small number of Sephardim settled in cities along the Atlantic coast of the American colonies, where they established themselves as successful merchants. Far greater numbers of Ashkenazim followed from Germany prior to the Civil War, and millions came subsequently, primarily Yiddish-speakers from what is loosely known as Eastern Europe. Many settled first in New York's Lower East Side, where most spoke Yiddish. (Yiddish is a vernacular language which is primarily German in content, but which also has extensive borrowings from Hebrew and various Slavic tongues.)

Most of these immigrants, who were largely barred from settling in the United States after World War I, were Orthodox in their religion, as opposed to the earlier Germans who often were inclined toward Reform. Jewish immigrants valued education highly, and by the second and third generations many had achieved considerable success in business, the professions, and academe. Following World War II, large Jewish communities developed in Miami, Los Angeles, and most larger cities.

Orthodox Jews today are divided into a number of communities who interpret their shared tradition considerably differently. Modern Orthodox Jews are fully comfortable in the contemporary world, and are not very distinguishable from Gentiles (non-Jews or, in Yiddish, *goyim*) in dress or general appearance. Like other Orthodox, however, they strictly observe traditional rules for worship and diet. *Haredim* are also strictly Orthodox and mixed in the secular world, but maintain some distinctly Old World practices, such as the wearing of distinctive black garb and hats as well as forelocks (a sort of exaggerated sideburn) by men.

Hasidism is another form of Orthodoxy that has been imported to this country from Europe following the Holocaust during World War II. Hasids are Orthodox Jews who organized around prominent rabbis during the eighteenth century and formed tight, distinctive communities characterized by mystical worship and dance. In the United States, they have arrived through collective emigration and re-formed their communities primarily in and around New York City, which has created controversy through their insistence on educating their own children in ways that do not conform to secular standards and similar isolationist practices.

The *Lubavitchers* are different in that they see themselves as missionaries to other Jews and try to evangelize them to bring them back to a stricter, more traditional form of Jewish life. They have established numerous centers on college campuses and in centers of Jewish population.

Worship and Ritual

See **Judaism Overview: Worship and Ritual**

Scriptures

See **Judaism Overview: Scriptures**

Common Misunderstandings, Stereotypes, and Classroom Concerns

See **Judaism Overview: Common Misunderstandings, Stereotypes, and Classroom Concerns**

Note

1   Pew Research Center Report on the U.S. 2020 Census, https://www.pewresearch.org/religion/2021/05/11/jewish-americans-in-2020/.

Further Reading and Resources

Lippy, Charles H., and Peter W. Williams, eds. *Encyclopedia of Religion in America*. Washington, DC: CQ Press, 2010, "Judaism: Conservative," 1114–1119; "Judaism: Jewish Culture," 1120–1124; "Judaism: Jewish Identity," 1125–1132; "Judaism: Jewish Science," 1133–1134; "Judaism: Orthodox," 1135–1140; "Judaism: Reconstructionist," 1141–1143; "Judaism: Reform," 1144–1149; "Judaism: Sectarian Movements," 1150–1152; "Judaism: Secular," 1153–1157; "Judaism: Tradition and Heritage," 1158–1168.

Sarna, Jonathan D. *American Judaism: A History*. New Haven, CT: Yale University Press, 2005.

38

Judaism: Reform

In 1883, Jewish leaders from all across the United States converged on Cincinnati to celebrate the first graduating class of Hebrew Union College, the nation's earliest rabbinical seminary. Isaac Mayer Wise, the school's founder and leader of the Reform movement in American Judaism, arranged for a gala banquet to be held at Cincinnati's Highland House. As the assembled guests, who represented a variety of strains within the American Jewish community, took their seats and awaited their dinner, outrage broke out as the waiters brought in the first course.

For Jews who observe tradition, among the first mandates they practice are the dietary laws set out in Chapter 11 of the book of *Leviticus*, which forbid the eating of pork and shellfish and the mixing of meat and milk products. The scandal of seeing dishes on the menu such as clams, shrimp, and crabs was immediately apparent to the observant, and led to the occasion's being dubbed the "Trayf (Trefa) Banquet." (Trayf in Hebrew means "unclean," the opposite of kosher/clean, suitable to eat.) It also precipitated the first major public rift within the heretofore loosely organized American Jewish community and the beginning of its division into formal denominations on the Protestant model.

Membership

Since American Jews differ considerably about exactly what constitutes a Jew, it is difficult to give precise numbers. The best available for the early 2020s are:[1]

> Total Jewish Population (including all who identify as Jewish in some way): 8,000,000 (2.4% of total U.S. population)
> Percentage Reform: 37% (3,000,000)
> Percent U.S. population: 2.4%

History

As the story of the Trayf Banquet illustrates, the tensions forming along the lines of tradition versus modernization for decades finally came to a head in the later nineteenth-century United States. This resulted in the organization of what had heretofore been a diffuse community of many persuasions now settling into distinct denominations on the Protestant model, sharing a common tradition but divided over what impact modern thought and society should play in the practice of this tradition in a pluralistic society.

The roots of Reform Judaism – note that "Reform" here is used as an adjective – lie in eighteenth-century Germany, where the philosopher Moses Mendelssohn, under the influence of Enlightenment thought, set about separating the essential core of Judaism from what he saw as outdated practices no longer applicable in a modernized, "enlightened" world. Some American Jewish congregations, beginning in the 1820s, began to adopt Mendelssohn's ideas, which included reforming worship on a Protestant model – adding sermons and organ music – while abandoning strict adherence to the kosher laws and seating segregated by sex. These ideas grew in popularity for the next several decades and became codified in the "Pittsburgh Statement" of 1885, which rejected the Mosaic (kosher) laws as well as Zionism, and affirmed that Judaism was a "progressive religion."

Isaac Mayer Wise helped to create an institutional infrastructure for American Reform, including a national rabbinical association, periodicals, and the Hebrew Union College. Reform became the most popular branch of American Judaism in the twentieth century, though the movement rejected its opposition to Zionism with the refounding of Israel. In later decades, Reform took the lead in permitting the ordination of women and gay people as rabbis, as well as permitting gay marriage.

Worship and Ritual

See **Judaism Overview: Worship and Ritual**

Scriptures

See **Judaism Overview: Scriptures**

Holidays and Festivals

See **Judaism Overview: Holidays and Festivals**

Common Misunderstandings, Stereotypes, and Classroom Concerns

See **Judaism Overview: Common Misunderstandings, Stereotypes, and Classroom Concerns**

Note

1 Pew Research Foundation Reporting on the 2020 U.S. Census, https://www.pewresearch.org/religion/2021/05/11/the-size-of-the-u-s-jewish-population/.

Further Reading and Resources

Lippy, Charles H., and Peter W. Williams, eds. *Encyclopedia of Religion in America*. Washington, DC: CQ Press, 2010, "Judaism: Conservative," 1114–1119; "Judaism: Jewish Culture," 1120–1124; "Judaism: Jewish Identity," 1125–1132; "Judaism: Jewish Science," 1133–1134; "Judaism: Orthodox," 1135–1140; "Judaism: Reconstructionist," 1141–1143; "Judaism: Reform," 1144–1149; "Judaism: Sectarian Movements," 1150–1152; "Judaism: Secular," 1153–1157; "Judaism: Tradition and Heritage," 1158–1168.

Sarna, Jonathan D. *American Judaism: A History*. New Haven, CT: Yale University Press, 2005.

39

Neo-Paganism

> In southwestern Minnesota, during a wedding ceremony a couple have their hands tied together with a decorative cord in a ritual act known as a "handfasting." Meanwhile, across the country in California, a high school student who has joined a witch's coven through a social media website meets online with her fellow members to help her visualize a successful outcome to a particularly stressful assignment. Across the Atlantic in the United Kingdom, a group meets near an ancient neolithic site to commune with the spirits of those they consider Druidic ancestors and discuss ways to protect those sites from potential development projects.

Introduction

The term "Neo-Paganism," or simply "Paganism," acts as an umbrella or catch-all term for a variety of practices and traditions. If any aspects can be said to connect or hold together the concept of "Paganism" as a group of traditions, one could point to a few items. First, there is a common perception (whether historically accurate or not, as we shall see) that the beliefs and practices are revitalizing or continuing customs or rituals dating back millennia. Second, most Pagan believers hold to a sense of immanent divinities or indeterminate forces at work in the natural world, linking together all life. In the following, we will touch on these few commonalities, as well as the differences between sub-traditions, and suggest ways instructors can be sensitive and welcoming to the concerns of Pagan students.

Historical Overview

The beginning of Pagan traditions can be traced back relatively recently to the early twentieth century. In 1929, scholar Margaret Murray published a study that posited a matriarchal, nature-based, pre-Christian religion across Europe in which witches were the central figures. Over time, the argument went, the encroachment and then dominance of the more patriarchal Christian tradition stamped out and demonized the nature-based religions, with the greatest persecution occurring during the early modern witch trials. A few decades later, in the 1940s, an Englishman named Gerald Gardner built on this scholarship to claim he had been initiated into a secret, still existent coven of witches belonging to this ancient tradition. Calling this tradition "Wicca," he created a text known as the *Book of Shadows* detailing its rituals and practices, which revolved around a powerful goddess figure and her consort, a horned god, who together represented the divinity of nature. Other interpretations of Wicca began to spread eventually, including ones focused entirely on goddess worship, as well as others concerned simply with nature, but less so with any divine figures. Continued scholarship over the years has largely refuted the claims of a pan-European witchcraft religion, but these revelations have not staunched the growth of Wicca or other Pagan traditions, who instead look at the story as a mythic or thematic presentation of the tension between the modern world and a state of greater connection to nature.

Simultaneously, starting in the mid-twentieth century, other movements were taking place in many parts of Europe that sociologists have connected to a reaction against the industrial, economic, and rational bent of the modern age. Max Weber, for instance, has termed the tendencies and motivations behind these movements as connected to a desire to "re-enchant" the world, to seek out or replace a certain magic or mystery the forces of modernity have driven from everyday life. These movements have been focused on revivals of ancient local traditions in the Baltic States of Eastern Europe, the Greek Isles, Great Britain, and Scandinavia, as a few examples. In Great Britain, for instance, this has taken the form of groups who have attempted to revitalize their vision of Druidic practices, while in Greece, there are those who see themselves as reinvigorating the spirit of the Olympian gods. Occasionally, in a trend which has continued to today, these groups at times cross over into nationalism, as they are interested in the supposed traditions that were practiced in a particular geographic location.

Despite the differences in origin and motivation, there are certain prominent similarities between Wiccan and Pagan movements at large. One is the emphasis on divine powers, to the extent these are named or considered, as being immanent and ever-present, even localized in oneself, as opposed to abstract or remote in a separate realm, such as a "heaven" or other dimension. It is within this context that the Wiccan tradition of casting spells should be concerned: an attempt, either alone or with the aid of others, to extend one's will into the strands that connect the various elements and forces of the world, to either attune oneself or attempt to impact an outcome or event.

A second commonality is the emphasis on a decentralized, non-hierarchical structure. Though Wicca and other Pagan groups may draw upon or look to certain important individuals, such as Gerald Gardner, as key figures, they are less likely to imbue them with any sense of absolute authority, and even less so see current figures as sources of expertise. Wicca and Paganism more broadly are rather individualistic, focusing on meaning found in practice as opposed to any supposed rightness in doctrine. Experience, often of nature and local surroundings, supersedes any sense of doctrine.

Third, as might be expected from the previous point, Pagan groups do not normally possess overarching ethical codes or structures. The most frequently cited code within Wicca, for instance, referred to sometimes as the "Wiccan rede," exhorts followers merely to act as they will, so long as it does not hurt others. Owing to the individualistic bent of Wicca, though, working out the parameters of this code is left to individuals.

Scriptures and Festivals

Owing to their non-hierarchical, decentralized nature, there are no universally agreed upon sacred scriptures or festivals found in Pagan traditions. Rather, texts and rituals are created and celebrated on a group-by-group, even individual-by-individual basis. A few overarching examples are possible, though, that cut across traditions. For one, initiation is a central practice in almost all Wiccan or Pagan groups, with emphasis placed on the manner in which an individual is brought into the fold, prior to allowing them to stamp their own identity onto the practice.

Additionally, especially for Pagan groups associated with a particular geographical, national area, the sense of place and locale is extremely important. For those updating and reviving ancient Latvian or Finnish practices, specific locations in each of those countries may be seen as sacred and become the site of pilgrimage or ritual. Graveyards filled with ancestors or places otherwise associated with ancient sites, such as Stonehenge in Great Britain, may serve as a locus of practice. For Wiccans, who might see nature itself as sacred, perhaps due to connection with the Great Goddess, this sacrality could be focused on a local nature area or transposed onto all of the natural world.

Across nearly all Pagan groups, owing to the emphasis on connection to the natural world, there is also an interest in rituals that honor the different facets of the calendar. Within Wicca, for example, many groups will conduct rituals or ceremonies for the solstices, the equinoxes, the beginning or end of the seasons, and other events connected to the turnings of the natural world. Sometimes referred to as the "Wheel of the Year," prominent examples of rituals and festivals (often termed "sabbats") include "Ostara" (in March), "Samhain" (late October or early November), and "Yule" (late December). For those Pagan groups associated with a particular nation, culture, or geography, these ceremonies might further take on a local emphasis or flavor.

Common Misunderstandings, Stereotypes, and Classroom Concerns

Witchcraft and Paganism can be subject to numerous misunderstandings. Particularly in more conservative regions and communities of the United States, the terms "witch" and "pagan," and the beliefs associated with them, can be misconstrued as related to what some Christian traditions consider demonic or Satanic. Members of Wicca and other Pagan groups have been subject to harassment due to this misunderstanding, so it is important to avoid or circumvent these associations whenever possible. Similarly, as noted above, though some Wiccan groups will celebrate Samhain around the time of the more commercially and civically prominent "Halloween," for Pagan groups, this is a calendrical festival associated with the changing of the seasons rather than the costume and treat-oriented celebration that is more culturally known in the United States. Additionally, again aside from the common perception and parlance, the Wiccan concept of "spellcasting," rather than invoking spirits or evil forces, we have seen above is much closer to the concept of visualization or even mindfulness, of attuning oneself to the world around, rather than beseeching external powers. Instructors should bear all these ideas and potential misconceptions in mind around Wiccan or Pagan students.

Culturally Responsive Pedagogy

In response to classroom concerns such as those stated above, instructors can take several steps to be responsive to Pagan or Wiccan students. For example, during the Halloween season, they can be sensitive to how the holiday is presented. Perhaps, if the Pagan or Wiccan student is willing and would not feel too put on the spot, they could discuss the ways in which their beliefs interpret the holiday, or do so during other periods of calendrical festivals at different points in the year. Also, for assignments, instructors can consider allowing or encouraging Pagan and Wiccan students to research the traditions of ancient Europe or other cultural connections to their beliefs, such as those found in older, per-Christian European traditions, or to include epics, narratives, or stories from a variety of places around the world, connected to the student's interest.

Further Reading and Resources

Adler, Margot. *Drawing Down the Moon: Witches, Druids, Goddess Worshippers, and Other Pagans in America Today*. New York: Penguin Books, 1986.

Aitamurto, Kaarina, and Scott Simpson. *Modern Pagan and Native Faith Movements in Central and Eastern Europe*. New York: Routledge, 2014.

Berger, Helen. *Witchcraft and Magic: Contemporary North America*. Philadelphia: University of Philadelphia Press, 2011.

Berger, Helen. *A Community of Witches: Contemporary New-Paganism and Witchcraft in the United States*. Columbia: University of South Carolina Press, 1999.

Davies, Owen. *Paganism: A Very Short Introduction*. Newy York: Oxford University Press, 2011.

Harvey, Graham. *Listening People, Speaking Earth: Contemporary Paganism*. London: Hurst Press, 2007.

Hutton, Ronald. *The Triumph of the Moon: A History of Modern Pagan Witchcraft*. New York: Oxford University Press, 1999.

Pike, Sarah. *Earthly Bodies, Magical Selves: Contemporary Pagans and the Search for Community*. Berkeley: University of California Press, 2001.

Schnurbein, Stefanie. *Norse Revival: Transformations of Norse Neopaganism*. Leiden: E.J. Brill, 2016.

Starhawk. *The Spiral Dance: A Rebirth of the Ancient Religion of the Great Goddess*. San Francisco, CA: Harper Collins, 1999.

Starhawk. *Truth or Dare*. New York: Harper and Row, 1990.

White, Ethan. *Wicca: History, Belief, and Community in Modern Pagan Witchcraft*. Chicago, IL: Sussex Academic Press, 2016.

York, Michael. *Pagan Theology: Paganism as a World Religion*. New York: New York University Press, 2003.

40

North American Indigenous Religions

> In the southeast of Alaska, a Tlingit community gathers 40 days after the death of one of its members to celebrate their life with stories and a meal. In the upper plains of the United States, protesters huddle in freezing cold temperatures near the Standing Rock Indian Reservation to protest the installment of the Dakota Access Pipeline (DAPL), which will cut across lands held sacred to numerous Native American nations. In the southwest of the United States, where the states of Arizona, Utah, Colorado, and New Mexico intersect, the Navajo people engage in ceremonial practices often adapted to contemporary concerns, such as the "Enemyway" ritual, which aims to restore the well-being of warriors and is now sometimes purposed to ameliorate the post-traumatic stress disorders suffered by military veterans.

Introduction

From the east to the west coast of the North American continent and the tip of Alaska to the Gulf of Mexico, the practices of indigenous communities consist of a staggering diversity of practices which both harken back to much older traditions but also greet the modern age in vibrant ways. Though settling on exact population figures is a challenge due to difficulties in procuring a completely accurate census, Native American populations number in several millions of individuals in the United States alone, consisting of nearly 600 distinct, federally recognized groups. Some of these groups have members only in the hundreds while the largest have much larger populations and span over wide ranges of territory. In this chapter, we will provide an overview of the few common ideas that might be found across these admittedly disparate and unique nations, being careful to provide specific examples where possible, then proceed on to the classroom concerns – and opportunities – that this diversity affords when instructors work with native peoples.

Historical Overview

Precisely how long and through what means human beings came to inhabit the North American continent is the subject of some controversy in archaeological circles. Many estimates suggest that humans first arrived in the Western hemisphere between 13,000 and 14,000 years ago, either by a land bridge then existing over what is now the Bering Strait, or perhaps by sea from Polynesian islands. Whichever the case may be, these first peoples soon spread across North America and founded complex, thriving civilizations from one end of the continent to the other.

Despite the aforementioned diversity of native traditions, a few very general commonalities can be found among most North American Indigenous cultures. The first is that there is often no clear or stark dividing line between religion and everyday life. In fact, some indigenous languages do not even possess a word corresponding to the distinct category or term "religion." The sacred is instead seen as a force around oneself at all times. For some groups, this means diffuse and individual spiritual powers inhabit the world, while for others there is a belief in an immanent yet also at times transcendent force in the world that enlivens and animates all existence. Among the latter, for the Lakota, this force is often referred to as *Wakan Tanka* while among the Iroquois, the term used is *Manitou*, and for their part, the Cheyenne call it *Maheo*. At times given personality and at times left amorphous, this force is an omnipresent and potent energy that must always be treated carefully and with the utmost respect, lest one come to harm. Harmony and balance are thus emphasized and reinforced as important values in order to maintain the correct outlook and behavior toward the spiritual forces around oneself and one's community.

Frequently, this notion of spirit extends to animals, as well as features of the landscape such as rocks, trees, rivers, and mountains, conferring a sense of personhood on all facets of the natural world. This in turn contributes to a concept of sacred geography where the practices and stories of many native communities are inextricably tied to their locality, where their religious tradition is an outgrowth and also a celebration of a specific landscape. In this way, many native traditions deftly weave grand cosmological beliefs into quite mundane circumstances.

For some indigenous groups, navigating relationships between the community and these powers is frequently the province of what scholars call "religious virtuosos" – those who know the proper rites and procedures to invoke or appease the forces of the world surrounding them and maintain the delicate balance of harmony with the spiritual world. As they mediate these powers for their community members, these figures serve as buffer zones for their people with the spirits around them. The actions undertaken in this role regularly correspond to what are called "life cycle rituals," which are practices around events that are commemorated in almost all cultures, such as childbirth, puberty, marriage, death, and other important occasions that mark some sort of important transition. Ceremonies and rituals may also coincide with bouts of personal illness or communal crisis at times when the natural balances or harmonies need to be restored or reinforced in the face of individual or community stress.

Finally, every indigenous community has been impacted by the experience of colonial settlement and attempted genocide, both cultural and literal. Native traditions have shown extraordinary resilience in the face of these historical pressures, persisting in the face of seemingly overwhelming odds. At times indigenous practices have developed to incorporate other traditions. A clear example can be found in the Tlingit Forty Day festival, described in the opening vignette, which melds Russian Orthodox ritual with native memorial practices. Importantly, this demonstrates the capacity of native peoples to adapt and change.

Holidays and Festivals

As opposed to certain other religious traditions across the world, such as Christianity or Islam, which emphasize written scripture, North American indigenous religious beliefs and practices, for most of their history, existed in oral form, passed down by word of mouth. Following European contact, colonists who encountered native cultures created their own written records of indigenous beliefs and practices with varying degrees of accuracy, until more recent times when anthropologists began compiling and interviewing surviving members of these nations. Unfortunately, it is difficult to ascertain what aspects of native traditions have already been lost given the disruption posed by colonialism.

In terms of festivals and holidays, due to the disparate forms of practice, this list includes only a select few from around the continent:

National Native American Heritage Day – Commemorated on the day after Thanksgiving, this civil holiday is considered a way to honor native traditions and highlight actual native practices as opposed to the caricatures that frequently abound during this time of year.

Indigenous People's Day – Since the late 1980s and early 1990s, this event has been celebrated in October in a number of states and localities as a counter to "Columbus Day." It is often commemorated with parades and marches.

Green Corn Ceremony – Representing the new year and new beginnings, this ceremony takes place over July and August in areas across the south and southeastern United States. The exact timing of the observance within the summer months depends on the growth of the corn crop and when the new ears of the eventual harvest emerge. Taking place over several days, the ceremony involves singing, dancing, and the kindling of a sacred fire.

Sun Dance – A key ceremony among Plains nations such as the Lakota and Cheyenne, the Sun Dance often takes place over the summer months of June to August. The community gathers to pray, sing, and dance around a pole, sometimes for lengthy periods of time as a test of endurance.

The examples above represent only a few holidays or festivals practiced by native peoples. Instructors are strongly encouraged to learn and discover the festivals, holidays, and practices of the native peoples in their local area so as to better know and reach out to the distinctive ways of belief and practice for their community.

Common Misunderstandings, Stereotypes, and Classroom Concerns

There are a number of potential misunderstandings and stereotypes surrounding North American indigenous religions. The first, as the foregoing has hopefully explored in this chapter, is that all such religions are the same and follow a monolithic pattern. While some broad commonalities may exist, Native American religions are also unique to each nation and possess remarkable differentiation. It is also helpful to avoid the stereotype of "spiritual, but not religious" that at times circulates around indigenous traditions since, though occasionally meant as a kind of counter-cultural compliment, these concepts can also be seen to render native peoples as "other" and even alien.

Similarly, the perception exists of native peoples as inherently eco-friendly or even as the first environmentalists. Though indigenous traditions often did (and do) advocate for a different relationship with the environment, one should also attempt to avoid the stereotype that all Native peoples always lived in complete harmony with nature and never impacted their surrounding ecosystem. This image of the completely environmentally friendly indigenous person can also be a way to render such communities as entirely "other."

A related stereotype sees indigenous peoples as products of the distant past and unaffected by change, whereas, as we have seen elsewhere in this chapter, Native American communities have undergone great periods of adaptation and change. Focusing too intently on ancient indigenous practices and traditions, though important historically, runs the risk of erasing the ways native peoples have persisted through often almost unendurable circumstances to create new ways of existing in and understanding the world.

One should also be wary of certain assumptions and terms. For example, any discussion of immigration to the United States (or even the inaccurate cliché that the country is a "nation of immigrants") should recognize that students of an indigenous background will relate to this topic differently. Similarly, one should be aware of prominent and persistent historical inaccuracies around native peoples, such as the holiday of "Thanksgiving" and the assertion that Christopher Columbus "discovered" America, and be prepared to use those as teachable moments to discuss the real role of indigenous communities in the history of the country. On that same point, some students' only exposure to Native Americans may have come through such misleading lenses as Disney films or sports mascots, which continue to portray native peoples as the "noble savage." It is important to anticipate and correct such ongoing and persistent stereotypes, which can even take the form of certain phrases or slang. An additional example of the latter is the term "spirit animal," which is frequently used in joking or levity and thus might be considered offensive by native peoples.

Within the classroom, an instructor should be careful not to misconstrue silence. When a student from an indigenous background is silent, this is not a sign of resistance or disrespect, but rather calm attention and even esteem. At the same time, instructors must also be aware of the difficult history behind the practice of education in the United States for indigenous peoples. Until relatively recently (even the 1970s), through government or Christian church-funded boarding schools, education was part and parcel of an attempt to eradicate indigenous cultural practices, beliefs, languages, and family structures.

Culturally Responsive Pedagogy

Any plan involving culturally responsive pedagogy related to indigenous communities must first and foremost take into account the specific local history, beliefs, and practices of the group involved. To the extent this is possible, one should become aware of the native community in one's school district or nearby area and seek ways in which their festivals, ways of knowing, stories, and mythologies can be brought into the classroom alongside those of other peoples. History, literature, science, and other curricula can all be enriched through contact with the local knowledge native groups can provide.

From another vantage, to the degree that they are comfortable, students of an indigenous background may be interested in researching and presenting their local history, or investigating and providing information on the inaccurate stereotypes and misconceptions discussed above. While obligating students to serve as the spokesperson for their communities should be avoided, should native students be interested in pursuing such projects, they may impart the lesson of the damage these portrayals propagate in far more effective ways than the instructor can.

Further Reading and Resources

Brown, Joseph Epes, and Emily Cousins. *Teaching Spirits: Understanding Native American Religious Traditions.* New York: Oxford University Press, 2010.

Crawford-O'Brien, Suzanne, and Inez Talamantez. *Religion and Culture in Native America.* New York: Rowan and Littlefield Press, 2020.

Crawford-O'Brien, Suzanne. *Native American Religious Traditions*. New York: Routledge Press, 2006.
Erdoes, Richard, and Alfonso Ortiz. *American Indian Myths and Legends*. New York: Pantheon Books, 1984.
Garbarino, Merwyn, and Robert Sasso. *Native American Heritage* (3rd ed.). Prospect Heights, IL: Waveland Press, 1994.
Gill, Sam. *Native American Religions: An Introduction* (2nd ed.). Belmont, CA: Wadsworth Publications, 2005.
Gill, Sam. *Native American Religious Action: A Performance Approach to Religion*. Charleston: University of South Carolina Press, 1987.
Lame Deer, John, and Richard Erdoes. *Lame Deer, Seeker of Visions*. New York: Simon and Schuster, 1994.
Martin, Joel. *The Land Looks After Us: A History of Native American Religion*. New York: Oxford University Press, 2001.
Sullivan, Lawrence, ed. *Native Religions and Cultures of North America: Anthropology of the Sacred*. New York: Continuum Press, 2000.

41

Scientology

> A ten-year-old girl from a family of Scientologists takes two metal probes that are attached to a device called an E-meter and responds to various questions in a session led by a church counselor. The counselor uses readings from the E-meter to assess how well the child is progressing along the Bridge to Total Freedom, the church's path of advancement. The child like all members of the church, aspires to reach a state known as "going clear."

Introduction

The church claims to have over 8 million members, but some critics estimate that actual numbers are as low as 20,000.[1] One can participate in Scientology at various levels, so this compounds the difficulty in knowing how many people practice the religion. Whatever the numbers, the church exercises an influence disproportionate to its size.

Historical Overview

Before landing on the term "Scientology," L. Ron Hubbard first created a therapeutic system he called "Dianetics." When the organization that he established in 1950 to promote this therapeutic system went bankrupt, Hubbard lost the rights to his book *Dianetics* in 1952. Hubbard pivoted at this point and described the therapeutic system as a religion. Hubbard founded the Church of Scientology in 1954.

The church teaches that traumatic events leave traces in the mind in the form of subconscious command-like recordings (termed "engrams") that can only be removed through a therapeutic process called "auditing." In auditing sessions, an auditor reads questions that the person being audited responds to while the auditor reads the E-meter device to see the extent to which engrams control the person's cognition. Once a person is deemed free of engrams, they are considered to be "clear." After attaining this status, Scientologists can take part in the "Operating Thetan" levels of the organization, which require further contributions to the church. Critics claim that practitioners of this religion have given hundreds of thousands of dollars to the organization.

Reincarnation is one of the core beliefs held by Scientologists. Practitioners believe that their past lives took place in extraterrestrial settings. There is a strong likelihood that when an adherent of the religion explores past lives, this process will reveal trauma. The church teaches that in the distant past, billions were harmed by nuclear weapons put in place by extraterrestrial overlords.

Common Misunderstandings, Stereotypes, and Classroom Concerns

Scientology is often dismissed as a cult. Obviously, children who practice the religion are sensitive to slurs about the religion and educators should avoid playing into stereotypes. Classroom activities that involve self-reflection and self-critique will likely play to the strengths of students who adhere to Scientology.

Note

1 Steinberg, Neil, "Give Scientology a Break: The Opening of a New Chicago Center Occasions Rehashing of Serious Accusations," *Chicago Sun Times*. March 10, 2024.

Further Reading and Resources

Gibney, Alex, director. *Going Clear: Scientology & the Prison of Belief*. Santa Monica, CA: HBO Documentary Films, 2015.

Henzel, Cynthia Kennedy. *Understanding Scientology*. Understanding World Religions and Beliefs. Minneapolis, MN: Essential Library, 2019.

Urban, Hugh B. *The Church of Scientology: A History of a New Religion*. Princeton, NJ: Princeton University Press, 2011.

42

Sikhism

> Members of a Sikh family living in Texas rise early on Sunday morning to organize the food that will be served at their temple that day. They do this to celebrate the birthday of their oldest boy. They have purchased all the foods that are to be served and will offer their time and energy to ensure that all who visit the temple that day will be able to enjoy a freshly made vegetarian meal.

Introduction

There are over 25 million Sikhs in the world.[1] This makes Sikhism the fifth-largest religion in the world. One in five people on the planet practice the religion: clearly the Sikh community has a considerable place in the world's religious landscape.

In the United States, Sikhs are not well understood. There is minimal teaching about the religion in U.S. schools. And, sadly, what is taught tends to be inaccurate. For example, many Americans would include Judaism when naming the major world religions. But there are more Sikhs than Jews in the world today, and yet Sikhism does not appear in many American world religion textbooks. Judaism generally does. The Sikh population is largely concentrated in South Asia, but Sikhs live all over the world. Outside of India and Pakistan, the next largest Sikh communities are in Canada, the United States, and the United Kingdom. There are significant Sikh communities in Southeast Asia and East Africa as well. Within America, the largest communities are concentrated on the two coasts, with the biggest populations in California, New York, and New Jersey. There are large Sikh communities in Vancouver and Ontario in Canada.

The oldest American Sikh place of worship was founded in 1912 in Stockton, California. If you were to travel across the United States, you'd find over 200 Sikh places of worship listed in the United States. The U.S. census doesn't ask about religion, so there is no precise data on the number of Sikhs in this country. Credible estimates range from about 300,000 to 700,000. Five hundred thousand, the number most commonly cited by the press, is a pretty good estimate of how many of your American neighbors are Sikhs.

Historical Overview

The history of the Sikh religion began in the Punjab region of northwestern India about 500 years ago. At this time, Muslims and Hindus were the predominant religious groups in North India. These groups were at loggerheads with each other over which religion would control state formations and exercise power. In 1469, a man who went by the name Nanak was born to a family of Hindus in a village in what is today's Pakistan. Spiritually inclined from a young age, Nanak was born into a Hindu merchant family, was educated, and took a job as a village accountant. He was married and had two sons. In his 20s, Nanak was in the habit of taking a ritualized bath in a river before dawn every morning, going to work during the day, and spending his evenings in the company of groups singing devotional songs. There was an egalitarian religious movement at the time that focused on devotion to God expressed in vernacular teachings, especially poetic compositions that uneducated people could sing. Nanak and a Muslim poet named Mardana were attracted to this movement and gravitated to those who composed songs that transcended the divide between Muslims and Hindus. Like others in his devotional circles, Nanak was disturbed by hidebound ways of practicing religion and critical of ways that religions in his locality legitimated social inequalities. One day when he was around 30 years old, Nanak had a transformative experience while bathing in a river. Beneath the surface of the river, Nanak had an ecstatic experience that lasted three days. Nanak's bathing companion searched frantically for him and declared his friend to be drowned. But Nanak emerged from the water eventually and spoke about his vision, beginning with the statement "there is neither Hindu nor Muslim." In one of his later hymns, Nanak describes the revelation that he received while under water. He was taken to the court of God. There Nanak was given divine nectar to drink and had an awe-inspiring experience of being in God's direct presence.

Nanak's life would never be the same. He left his hometown and traveled in the company of the bard Mardana for 20 years. In the process of wandering from place to place, composing songs of praise, and learning songs composed by others (including Hindus and Muslims), Nanak established a new religion that in the Punjabi language is known as Sikhi and in the English language is generally known as Sikhism. Westerners are often embarrassed to pronounce the word "Sikh" in the Punjabi style: it sounds like the English word "sick," although the final consonant is more akin to the "ch" Scottish word "loch" than the "ck" in "luck."

Eventually, Nanak founded a town in central Punjab, in the heart of farming country, and tended crops as a way to make a living and commune with the One. Those who joined Nanak called him Guru Nanak and learned to recognize the divine presence in all aspects of life, including work. Guru Nanak taught by example, showing that even the most humble forms of manual labor offer a chance to enhance one's devotion. Engaging in fair and honest business practices offered early Sikhs a way to overcome egoism and cultivate love of the divine in the everyday. Following the example of the early community, Sikhs today live their spirituality through work. It's said that when Guru Nanak was deciding who to appoint as his successor, he purposely did not choose the son who was inclined to ascetic self-discipline. He preferred the son who found meaning in honest work.

Sikhs say that Guru Nanak received revelation directly from God and transmitted it in hymns that can be chanted and sung. The hymns exhort humans to revere a single divine being who created this world and lives within it, especially in the God-centered human heart. The central problem that the Sikhi religion overcomes is one that also concerns Hindus, Buddhists, and Jains: the cycle of reincarnation. Sikhs say that humans can break free of the cycle by shaking off the power of their egos and basking in the radiance of the One. God is equally present in all people, but cannot be confined to any physical form. God lives within the human heart. In his breakthrough experience under water, Nanak learned to proclaim the Divine Name (*nam*) – a term that refers to everything in the universe, both what is within us and outside us. Just as for Hindus the sacred syllable om contains all, so for Sikhs "nam" suggests the sacred power of incantatory language that animates everything in the universe. Nanak taught that meditation on the name can lead a person to liberation from the cycle of birth and death.

Sikhs revere a God who is both abstract and present on earth. There are many ways of speaking of God in Sikh scripture; different sects and different eras of Sikh history offer different options for speaking of God. The most common term for God in modern Sikhi is *Waheguru*, a Punjabi term which might be translated as "wondrous" (*wahe*) teacher or "enlightener" (*guru*). A particularly snappy translation is "wow guru." The word "guru" is central to the embodied theology of the religion. Waheguru is without physical form. And yet this is a God that one can establish a personal relationship with by following the teachings of Nanak and the nine subsequent gurus in his lineage. Sikhs follow the ways of the gurus in striving to live up to three daily principles each day: truthful living, service to humanity, and devotion to the divine. Sikhs practice service (reverent and focused action) as a way of expressing gratitude to the divine. The term for this love-inspired service is *seva*. All Sikhs are expected to serve humanity as a way of rebuilding one's core around divine love rather than ego.

Scripture and Worship

The central scripture that is the focus for Sikh learning and devotion is the *Guru Granth Sahib* (also called the *Adi Granth*). It is a collection of over 3,000 hymns composed by Nanak, his successors, and other spiritual figures, including Hindus and Muslims. The inclusion of writings by poet saints of other religions indicates the pluralistic nature of the Sikh religion: Sikhs believe that Sikhi is not the only way to cultivate divine love. In the way that Sikhs worship today, it's clear that Sikhs follow what might be called the sonic theology of Guru Nanak. The central focus of worship is the recitation of the scripture's hymns of praise, generally set to music. The place of worship is called a gurdwara, meaning "door to the guru." Entering a gurdwara, one's eye is drawn to the center of the main hall. There, in the central place that an altar might be placed in a Christian church or a sculpture of a deity might occupy in a Hindu temple, Sikhs genuflect in front of the scripture. Sikhs and visitors who worship at the gurdwara place their foreheads on the carpeted floor to show their devotion, offer a small amount of cash in a donation box, then sit down and absorb the hymns. Some sway along with the music that accompanies the hymns of praise. Sacred sound connects the majesty of Waheguru with the rhythms of life in the body, gives young children a model to follow, and helps the congregation to remember the divine and kindle divine love.

Sikhs believe that this holy book is the last of the gurus in the line of succession that began with Guru Nanak. It is a guru-in-book-form; the name *Guru Granth Sahib* translates in English as "respected guru book." The sacred book is treated with the same respect and reverence that one would show Guru Nanak or one of his successor gurus. Each day, the book is woken up (as one would gently wake a visiting guest). Each morning at 5:30 a.m., an attendant whose job is to care for the guru-in-book-form opens the holy book at random and reads the opening words of the hymn at the top of the left-hand page. This daily guidance is posted on a board in the foyer of each Sikh worship center. The holy text is treated like royalty. Just as a royal figure in a north Indian court would be made comfortable in India's hot climate in the days before electric fans and air conditioning by the breezes generated by an attendant waving a fan, so the guru–in-book-form has an attendant who works with a fan made from the tail of a yak or a horse to keep the air moving as long as the book is open. The book rests on a cushioned stand under a canopy during the day. Each night, the *Guru Granth Sahib* is ceremoniously closed, wrapped, and laid to rest in a small room outside the main worship hall.

Most Sikhs have handbooks in their homes that contain scriptural passages used in daily prayer. Sikhs in America and elsewhere hear the scriptures by listening to audio via the Internet and via Punjabi television channels. Few Sikhs are able to provide the set-aside spaces and dedicated time needed to keep a copy of the *Guru Granth Sahib* at home. Those who want to do so must create a gurdwara-like room separate from other rooms and ensure that the book is opened in the morning and placed in a space for rest in the evening. Some Sikhs hold that a home with alcohol in it is not a home that should house a *Guru Granth Sahib*. Vegetarian food is also a sign of respect that marks proper reverence for the scripture. When religious rituals are performed at a Sikh home, the scripture is wrapped in cloth and carefully carried from a gurdwara. It will be treated with utmost reverence and respect. So while the scripture is carried to the home, only strictly vegetarian food should be cooked and served. Someone sprinkles water on the ground in front of the person bearing the scripture. For the last few steps, the person who carries the *Guru Granth Sahib* carries the book on their head. Once the holy book is installed in the home under a canopy as it would be in a gurdwara, care is taken that no one on the second floor of the house walks directly over it.

Every gurdwara has a community kitchen that serves free vegetarian meals to anyone who wishes to eat, no matter their background, caste, religion, or socio-economic status. Guru Nanak created the practice of a daily communal meal, called langar, that shows in a vivid way how Sikhs dedicated themselves to selfless service and eliminating the hierarchies that too often divide people in society. People sit down on the floor to share a meal. During the founder's time, social hierarchies were reflected in seating arrangements, with people higher up in the social hierarchy seated above their social inferiors. By having everyone sit together on the floor, the meal ritual transmits a clear message of equality. Volunteers prepare the langar meal. Normally at American gurdwaras, different families sign up in advance. When the time comes in the schedule, family members bear the expense of purchasing food and spearhead the preparation of the langar meal.

After Guru Nanak's death, Sikhism grew more established under the guidance of subsequent gurus. As the Sikhs expanded their base of power in Punjab, confrontation with the imperial power of the Mughal Empire resulted. Accusations of sedition, imprisonment, and execution ended the life of the fifth guru. The ninth and tenth gurus encountered restrictive policies under Mughal emperors. Islamic laws imposed on non-Muslims, taxes on non-Muslims, and the replacement of Hindu temples with mosques led the tenth guru to a stance of active resistance. He proclaimed the right of Hindus to practice their religion without interference and he refused to accept Islam. These stances ultimately led to the tenth guru's imprisonment and execution. Before he died, the tenth guru created a new institution that would give the religion the stability needed to survive trying times, even without another guru to succeed him. The tenth guru called on all Sikhs in 1699 to gather in the city of Anandpur on Vaisakhi, the day that traditionally marked the celebration of the harvest festival in Punjab. On this occasion, the tenth guru asked who would step forward to offer absolute loyalty in defense of Sikh values, even to the point of death. Those fearless individuals resolute in their commitment to a Sikh way of life formed an initiated community called the Khalsa. The Khalsa offered a formal structure that would survive the death of the tenth guru. Without the need to appoint a human successor, the tenth guru declared that the *Guru Granth Sahib* would take his place and give guidance to the community. Using a straight-sword, the guru and his wife stirred sugar wafers into water in an iron vessel while reciting sacred verses, then offered this sweetened water as *amrit*, the nectar of immortality to those gathered for initiation. One after another, the initiates drank from the edge of the vessel, impervious to the worries about religious impurity carried in a lower-caste person's saliva that were common in early modern India. In this way, a brotherhood of equals was created. In the tenth guru's day, it was only men who took initiation and formed the Khalsa. But this initiation is available to both men and women today. Men who undergo initiation are given the title Singh ("lion"), while women are given the title Kaur ("princess"). Sikhs refer to those who have joined the Khalsa as *Amrit-dharis* ("those who bear the nectar"). It's also common to hear initiated Sikhs referred to as "baptized" Sikhs.

For those who have joined the Khalsa, five distinctive articles of faith show one's commitment to the values of the religion.

1. *Kesh* (uncut hair). Male and female members of the Khalsa refrain from cutting any hair on the body. Long hair represents a disciplined life that's focused on Waheguru. Combing it carefully and keeping it clean show reverence for the gift of the human body that God created. For men, combing the hair, tying it in a topknot, and covering it with a cloth indicates a disciplined holiness. Adult males (and some females) wear turbans. Younger Sikhs (males and sometimes females) wear *patkas*, a smaller head covering that uses less cloth and requires less time and effort to tie.
2. *Kanga* (wooden comb). Sikhs always carry a small wooden comb. It is needed to keep the hair neat and clean; it symbolizes one's respect for the gift of the body and the discipline required to care for it properly.
3. *Kara* (steel bracelet). Sikhs wear a circular steel bracelet on the wrist. This custom originated as a way to avoid getting one's hand cut off in a sword fight. But the symbolism of the bracelet goes deeper than mere self-defense: it stands for unity with God and the concept of eternity.
4. *Kirpan* (ceremonial sword): Sikhs carry a very small ceremonial sword that symbolizes the duty to fight for justice and protect the innocent.

5. *Kachera* (cotton underwear): This is a cotton undergarment that resembles boxer shorts. This style of underwear represents one's commitment to modesty and controlling physical desires.

Holidays

1. Guru Nanak Gurpurab (or Guru Nanak's Birthday): One of the most important Sikh festivals, celebrating the birth of Guru Nanak, the founder of Sikhism. The holiday usually occurs in October or November, according to the Gregorian calendar.
2. Vaisakhi (Baisaki) is commemorated by Sikhs annually in mid-April. This spring holiday celebrates the fertility of the harvest. It also marks the birthday of the Khalsa, giving the community a chance to celebrate the creation of a group that infused the religion with new life at a time when it could easily have ended. In the United States, those who wish to take initiation into the Khalsa often choose this holiday as the occasion to do so. Reenacting the ritual that was performed by the tenth guru and his wife, initiates receive the sweetened water administered with the invocation of sacred verses and take the articles of faith as a daily practice going forward.
3. Guru Gobind Singh Birthday: This holiday commemorates the birth of Guru Gobind Singh, the tenth guru who established the Khalsa and made many other contributions to the survival of the religion. It usually falls in December or January.
4. Guru Arjan Martyrdom: This holiday marks the martyrdom of the fifth Guru of Sikhism, said to have been killed in 1606. It is observed in June.
5. Guru Tegh Bahadur Martyrdom: This holiday marks the death of the ninth Guru of Sikhism, who gave his life for the freedom of religion. It is observed in November.

6. Bandi Chhor Divas: This festival is celebrated to mark the release of the sixth Guru of Sikhism, from imprisonment along with several other Hindu kings who were imprisoned by Muslim authorities. The holiday usually coincides with the festival of Diwali that is celebrated by Hindus, Jains, Sikhs, and others.
7. Martyrdom of the Sahibzadas: This day remembers the martyrdom of the four sons of the tenth guru. It falls in December.
8. Maghi: This holiday marks the martyrdom of those who died defending the tenth guru.

Common Misunderstandings, Stereotypes, and Classroom Concerns

Due to ignorance about Asian religions, many Americans cannot tell the difference between a Sikh and a Muslim. Both religions are practiced by ethnic South Asians; both feature religious head coverings worn by some adults. After 9/11/2001, many Sikh Americans were attacked by those who bore ill will against Muslims. Another common misunderstanding is the belief that Sikhs carry dangerous weapons. Far from being a threat, the *kirpan* that many Sikhs carry is a small, dull knife. It is often sewn into a knife-holder, hence unlikely to pose any danger.

Note

1 This population estimate is drawn from research done by the Pew Research Center. "The Global Religious Landscape." December 18, 2012, https://www.pewresearch.org/religion/2012/12/18/global-religious-landscape-exec/#:~:text=The%20demographic%20study%20%E2%80%93%20based%20on,the%20world%20as%20of%202010.

Further Reading and Resources

Jhutti-Johal, Jagbir. *Sikhism Today*. London and New York: Continuum, 2011.

Singh, Simran Jeet. *Sikhism: A Reporter's Guide*. The Sikh Coalition, Columbia, Missouri: Religion News Foundation, 2021. www.sikhcoalition.org/wp-content/uploads/2018/01/Sikhism-Reporters-Guide-Electronic.pdf. Accessed 9 July 2024.

Singh, Nikky-Guninder Kaur. *Sikhism: An Introduction*. London: Tauris, 2011.

43

Zoroastrianism

> In Yazd, Iran, a crowd gathers near a roaring flame, making offerings and praying to the Wise Lord above. Meanwhile, in Mumbai, India, a family discusses the plans for the funeral of a loved one and the proper way to handle their remains: should they be dealt with as the tradition has advised since ancient times, interred in the dakhma tower, or given over to more modern treatment such as burial or cremation? Continents away, in a Fire Temple in Pomona, New York, a young man is officially initiated into his community through the tying of the sacred thread around his ceremonial shirt. Across the world, the Zoroastrian religious tradition continues to meld ancient ways into modern times and places.

Introduction

Zoroastrianism is one of the oldest religions in the world, tracing back several thousand years to the central Asian plateau of what is now modern-day Iran and neighboring countries. It is also one of the smallest traditions referred to as a world religion, with between only 100,000 and 200,000 adherents. Most of these practitioners are found in India and Iran, though communities are also found in the United Kingdom and the United States. In the following, we will discuss the main beliefs of this tradition, outline a few of its primary scriptures and festivals, and cover classroom concerns and connections to pedagogy.

Historical Overview

Zoroastrian history can be traced back at least to the second millennium BCE. Although the exact time period of his life is uncertain, most scholars trace the life of Zoroastrianism's founder, Zarathushtra, to around 1200 BCE. The Greek version of his name ("Zoroaster") was popularized, leading to the name given to the tradition. The fundamental principle of the religion is a stark dualism between the forces of good and evil, light and darkness, truth and lies, and purity and corruption. In Zoroastrian thought, the high god Ahura Mazda is opposed by the demonic evil spirit Angra Mainyu. From Ahura Mazda, all good and pure elements of life flow, including the earth itself, water, plants, animals, and humans. Out of hatred and jealousy, Angra Mainyu and his malignant minions attempt to attack and corrupt all that the high god creates. Disease, death, and all other manner of negative elements of life arise from the influence and destructive polluting power of Angra Mainyu and his forces.

In response, the primary goal in a Zoroastrian's life is to take a stand in this conflict and side in all things with Ahura Mazda, doing good deeds, saying good words, and maintaining good thoughts. Zoroastrians believe that at some point in the future, the conflict between Ahura Mazda and Angra Mainyu will finally be resolved, with the high god defeating his demonic adversary and destroying evil forever. This end-of-times event, involving the resurrection and judgment of the dead, has frequently been compared to similar ideas in the traditions of Judaism and Christianity. In addition, some scholars believe that the concepts of angels as well as heaven and hell in later Western religions ultimately stemmed originally from Zoroastrianism.

As a consequence of this ongoing battle between cosmic forces of good and evil, Zoroastrians believe they are called to preserve truth, act ethically in the world, and maintain purity as ways of showing their devotion to Ahura Mazda. A symbol of this purity is found in the flames kept burning in the ceremonial fires of Zoroastrian temples. Key Zoroastrian ceremonies involve prayers and offerings before these fires, while one of the ongoing obligations of the Zoroastrian priestly institution is to tend to and keep these ritual fires. Zoroastrians believe that at the time of death, one's conduct in life is judged as the soul must traverse what is called the Chinvat Bridge. Those who have chosen to follow Ahura Mazda and maintain goodness in thought, word, and deed will pass the bridge easily, while others will fall and be punished.

From its place of origin in central Asia, Zoroastrianism was brought into what is now modern-day Iran by nomadic peoples. Starting with the founding of the Achaemenid Empire around the sixth century BCE, the tradition became the state religion of the empire and spread from the Mediterranean Sea to the western areas of modern India. The situation changed with the rise of Islam in southwest Asia, eventually leading to the migration of many Zoroastrians from Persia/Iran to India around the tenth century of the common era. Today, this is where most practitioners and communities now live, although some remain in Iran. The Zoroastrian population in India is frequently referred to by the term "Parsi," most likely derived from "Persian," the land of their ancestors' origin. Zoroastrians in Iran are sometimes called "Iranis" and there occasionally are differences in terminology and ritual calendars between the two groups. In some ways, especially since tradition has held that marriages should only take place within the community and between fellow Zoroastrians, the lines between religious tradition and ethnic identity are often blurred. Related to this, over time among many Zoroastrians, there has been an emphasis on marriage only within the community, which is a potential factor for the dwindling number of practitioners in the world.

Scriptures and Festivals

A text known as the *Avesta* is the primary scripture in Zoroastrianism. This text is composed of multiple subdivisions including the *Yasna*, which contains rules and instructions for ritual recitations. A further subdivision of the *Yasna* itself, the *Gathas*, comprise hymns of praise to Ahura Mazda and the minor celestial figures who follow and assist the high god.

Zoroastrians celebrate many seasonal festivals called Gahanbars throughout the year associated with each of the elements of Ahura Mazda's creation. For example, the spring festival of Maidyozarem Gahanbar celebrates the end of winter and the return of life. Other festivals more specifically celebrate harvest, animals, and human beings, since each was considered pure due to the creation of Ahura Mazda prior to the evil intervention of Angra Mainyu. Since different Zoroastrian communities around the world follow different calendars, the exact dates of observances differ depending on the particular group. Zoroastrians also frequently celebrate the New Year, known as Nouruz, and the birthday of Zarathushtra, called Khordad Sal.

Besides seasonal festivals and celebrations, Zoroastrian communities also commemorate life cycle rituals. For Parsis, between the ages of seven and ten, children are initiated formally into the tradition in a ritual known as the navjote. For Iranis, the ritual is referred to as sedreh pushi and occurs when the child is a teenager. During this ceremony, a priest consecrates and bestows a sacred thread or rope upon the initiated, which is then tied around their shirt three times. The thread is a reminder of the believer's obligation to follow Ahura Mazda in doing good actions, telling the truth, and thinking good thoughts.

Another life cycle ritual key to Zoroastrian belief is the observance of prohibitions surrounding the bodies of the deceased. Corpses are seen as highly impure and polluting, and Zoroastrians are required to dispose of them in a manner that is least likely to contaminate the pure creations of Ahura Mazda, namely earth, plants, fire, and water. In traditional communities and more ancient times, this often involved a structure called a dakhma, a high tower where corpses were left to be cleansed by scavenging animals, thus avoiding contact with soil, fire, and water. Although a few such towers still exist, for instance in areas around Mumbai in India, modern health codes, zoning laws, and neighborhood concerns frequently impede the contemporary use of dakhmas for the disposal of the dead. As a result, many Zoroastrian communities have adapted to changing times by adopting cremation or modified forms of burial to care for the bodies of deceased members.

Common Misunderstandings, Stereotypes, and Classroom Concerns

An instructor in a classroom containing Zoroastrian students can first make these students more comfortable by seeking out more information about the tradition. Since this is usually a lesser-known religion, demonstrating basic knowledge can often be of great assistance and several sources providing more details and overview are included in the "Further Reading and Resources" section. Related to this, if a student is from India or Iran, it is helpful to be open to the possibility that they are Zoroastrian as opposed to another tradition from those parts of the world.

More specifically, instructors should be aware of the Zoroastrian stance on purity and the ways in which it may impact student behavior or needs. Objects often seen as impure within the tradition include hair, finger, and toenails when detached from the body, and also breath, saliva, and blood. Like a corpse, these substances are seen as extensions of Angra Mainyu's attack on the pure creation of Ahura Mazda. Students may require assistance and understanding in situations that arise in the classroom involving these substances, such as the opportunity to adjourn to the restroom to wash and repurify themselves.

Another aspect to be aware of regarding Zoroastrianism is its aforementioned connections to ethnic identity. Along with this, tension between older and younger members of the community are sometimes apparent, with some who might be Parsi as an ethnic identification, but do not necessarily practice the rituals or adhere to the cosmological elements of the tradition.

Culturally Responsive Pedagogy

Students from Zoroastrian traditions, since the roots of the religion originate in ancient Persia, may appreciate connections to history and literature from that region, which frequently tends to be emphasized less in curricula. Alongside epics such as *The Odyssey* from the Greek tradition, literature or history courses could also discuss or even read portions of the *Shanamah*, the Persian epic of the hero Rustam. Similarly, from a point of view originating in ancient Persia, figures in history are sometimes seen differently. A prime example is the Macedonian king Alexander, often referred to as "Alexander the Great." Since many of his victories took place over the Persian army and his forces destroyed many Persian cities, he has often been called "Alexander the Accursed," from that perspective. Considering these sorts of issues will help in being culturally responsive to Zoroastrians in the classroom.

Further Reading and Resources

Boyce, Mary. *Zoroastrians: Their Religious Beliefs and Practices*. New York: Routledge, 2000.
Boyce, Mary. *Textual Sources for the Study of Zoroastrianism*. Chicago, IL: University of Chicago Press, 1990.
Boyce, Mary. *A History of Zoroastrianism*. Leiden: Brill, 1982.
Clark, Peter. *Zoroastrianism: An Introduction to an Ancient Faith*. Liverpool: Liverpool University Press, 1998.
Kriwaczek, Paul. *In Search of Zarathustra: Across Iran and Central Asia to Find the World's First Prophet*. New York: Vintage Press, 2004.
Mehr, Farhang. *The Zoroastrian Tradition*. Costa Mesa, CA: Mazda Publishers, 2003.

Nigosian, Solomon Alexander. *The Zoroastrian Faith: Tradition and Modern Faith*. Buffalo, NY: McGill-Queen's University Press, 1993.
Rose, Jenny. *Zoroastrianism: An Introduction*. London: I.B. Tauris, 2011.
Rose, Jenny. *Zoroastrianism: A Guide for the Perplexed*. New York: Continuum, 2011.
Zaehner, Robert Charles. *The Dawn and Twilight of Zoroastrianism*. New York: Putnam Press, 1961.

For Product Safety Concerns and Information please contact our EU
representative GPSR@taylorandfrancis.com
Taylor & Francis Verlag GmbH, Kaufingerstraße 24, 80331 München, Germany

www.ingramcontent.com/pod-product-compliance
Lightning Source LLC
Chambersburg PA
CBHW062139300426
44115CB00012BA/1987